B-26 INVADER
UNITS OVER KOREA

OSPREY AVIATION

OSPREY FRONTLINE COLOUR

4

B-26 INVADER
UNITS OVER KOREA

Warren Thompson

First published in Great Britain in 2000 by Osprey Publishing
Elms Court, Chapel Way, Botley, Oxford, OX2 9LP

ISBN 1 84176 080 3

Edited by Tony Holmes
Page design by Mark Holt
Cutaway Drawing by Mike Badrocke
Origination by Grasmere Digital Imaging, Leeds, UK
Printed through Bookbuilders, Hong Kong

00 01 02 03 04 05   10 9 8 7 6 5 4 3 2 1

EDITOR'S NOTE

To make the Osprey Frontline Colour series as authoritative as
possible, the Editor would be interested in hearing from any
individual who may have relevant information relating to the
aircraft, units and aircrew featured in this, or any other, volume
published by Osprey Aviation. Similarly, comments on the edito-
rial content of this book would also be most welcomed by the
Editor. Please write to Tony Holmes at 10 Prospect Road,
Sevenoaks, Kent, TN13 3UA, Great Britain, or by e-mail at:
tony.holmes@osprey-jets.freeserve.co.uk

For a catalogue of all books published by Osprey
Military and Aviation please write to:

**The Marketing Manager, Osprey Direct, PO Box
140, Wellingborough, Northants, NN8 4ZA, UK
E-mail: info@ospreydirect.co.uk**

**The Marketing Manager, Osprey Direct USA,
PO Box 130, Sterling Heights, MI 48311-0310, USA
Email: info@OspreyDirectUSA.com**

Visit Osprey at **www.ospreypublishing.com**

FRONT COVER *It is early morning at Kunsan (K-8), and the first
stages of the daily turnaround have already begun. The crew
chiefs for each aircraft have the previous pilots' post-sortie
maintenance 'write-ups' to hand, and they have all day to rectify
the minor 'gripes' and then fine tune their charges ready for the
night mission that lay ahead. The ordnance crews will arrive mid-
afternoon to load each Invader with its unique bombload, which
has been specifically tailored to fulfil each aircraft's individual
mission requirement – the B-26 could accurately dispense a wide
range of weapons. These Invaders belong to the 3rd Bomb Wing's
13th Bomb Squadron. One of the most successful outfits in Korea,
the 3rd BW destroyed in excess of 31,000 vehicles with the B-26
(Ray Anastos)*

BACK COVER *Having completed a mission to the Chosin
Reservoir, 1Lt Stan Weidman wearily extricates himself from the
cockpit of his Invader at the end of a long flight back to his base
at Miho, in Japan. This photograph was taken in December 1950,
shortly after Weidman had arrived in-theatre with the USAF
Reserve-manned 452nd BW. Hailing from California, the new
wing effectively doubled the number of Invader units committed
to the Korean War upon its assignment to the Far East Air Force.
The 452nd arrived in Japan with four B-26 units, although it soon
transferred one of these to the 3rd BW (Stan Weidman)*

TITLE PAGE *Pilot Lt Guy Brown poses with his mount at Miho AB
soon after the 452nd BW had arrived in Japan. Previously located
at Long Beach Airport, the wing was staffed predominantly by
Californian reservists, most of whom were World War 2 veterans.
The 452nd's west coast flavour was reflected in the large number
of Californian place names assigned to the wing's B-26s, and
PASADENA PISTOL PACKER II was no exception (Guy Brown)*

TITLE VERSO PAGE *The B-26's legendary Norden bombsight of
World War 2 fame dominates this unusual view of a 13th BS
Invader at K-8 in March 1953. The sight proved to be useful for
only a brief period during the Korean conflict, as B-26 units
quickly switched from day to night operations. However, prior to
this the Norden had been most effective during the large
formation bomb drops that were carried out in daylight against
suspected ammo dumps and rail complexes (Corky Sumner)*

CONTENTS

LEFT *Photographed several months after the Korean War had ended, this formation of 8th BS B-26s is seen Japan-bound for a spell of well-earned R&R. On 5 October 1954, both the 8th and 13th FBSs moved from Kunsan to Johnson AB, in Japan (Roy Degan)*

INTRODUCTION

For roughly a quarter of the 20th Century, the United States found itself in armed conflict. However, only two of these periods were deemed world wars, with the remaining actions being politically driven and, for the most part, unpopular with the public. In 1950, the newly-formed United Nations (UN) was put to the test in Korea, with its very credibility being at stake. This essentially civil war ended with a line 'drawn' just about where it had started, with little ground gained by either side and seemingly nothing accomplished by the UN forces sent to counter the communist armies attacking from the north. However, nothing could be farther from the truth.

South Korea had retained its independence, with its elected government intact and its geographical borders essentially as they had been prior to the invasion by North Korea.

Although large battles had been waged on the ground between UN and communist troops, the significant victories won by the forces backing South Korea had been accomplished through the use of airpower. UN pilots had taken on the very capable MiG-15s, flown by their Soviet and/or Warsaw Pact counterparts, and achieved air supremacy both over the battlefield and deep into North Korea itself. Should they have failed in their task, the war's outcome might have been dramatically different for both South Korea and the UN.

In June 1950, the Far East Air Force (FEAF) was grossly undermanned both in terms of aircraft and aircrew. With the exception of new F-80s being brought into theatre to replace the F-51 Mustang, there were few aircraft immediately available to counter the surprise North Korean invasion of the south. In the wake of the communist thrust, US forces were hastily reinforced to the point where they could counter the 'juggernaut' that threatened to engulf the Korean peninsula.

As strange as it may seem, during the first weeks of the war the F-80 proved ineffective due to its limited range. It was therefore left to obsolescent World War 2 piston-engined types such as the F-51 and B-26 to buy the UN forces the time needed to bolster their ranks.

FEAF Bomber Command had just one bomb group of B-26s (the 3rd BW) in the Far East when war broke out, and it was under strength with only two squadrons assigned. The only other dedicated bomber asset in-theatre was a single group of B-29s based at Kadena AB, on Okinawa. This meagre force was never going to be enough to repel the invading communist armies.

As the war progressed, the number of B-29 bomb groups quickly increased from one to five, and they proceeded to level all of the strategic targets in North Korea in just a matter of months in late 1950. Two of these groups were withdrawn right before the Chinese entered the war in November 1950.

Although the strategic bombers had effectively completed their role in the conflict by the end of 1950, the tactical B-26 would remain in heavy demand from day one through to the signature of the truce in July 1953. The maximum number of Invader groups available to the FEAF during the war never exceeded two, each of which was comprised of three squadrons. Their tasking was probably the most pressure-packed of any outfit, or aircraft type, in-theatre due to the fact that most Invader missions were flown at night.

The key to restricting the enemy from gaining any ground was to take away his ability to mount an effective offensive. This meant that communist supply routes had to be stopped or interrupted. After the first few weeks of the war, it became apparent to the North Koreans that nothing could be moved in daylight because of the large number of UN fighter-bombers that roamed freely overhead, looking for targets to attack. When the Chinese entered the war they too moved supplies at night, and they would prove worthy opponents for the B-26.

Despite the seemingly impenetrable nature of the rugged terrain that predominated in North Korea, B-26 crews regularly navigated down to tree-top level at night to fly through valleys at top speed in search of truck convoys and trains. They performed this hazardous mission night after night with great success, and their efforts were instrumental in halting the numerically superior Chinese Army from gaining any significant ground south of the 38th Parallel.

While this volume focuses on the Invader's successes, one should never forget that the price paid for stalemate at the front was extremely high, both in terms of aircrew and aircraft lost. Those that went down deep in North Korea were never heard from again, and exactly what happened on those missions will never be known. They took off from their bases and never returned.

This volume is dedicated to their memory.

Warren E Thompson
Germantown, Tennessee
June 2000

OPPOSITE *Typical of the elaborate paint jobs applied to the war-weary B-26Cs in Korea was* RUSH'S RENEGADES/HOT TO TROT!, *which was the personal mount of the commanding officer of the 8th BS, Lt Col Rush. It was photographed between missions at Kunsan in late 1952 (Robert Fortney)*

CHAPTER ONE
ROLE EXPANSION

BELOW *This prewar photograph shows the 3rd BW's flightline at Yokota AB, Japan. These B-26Bs are all hard-nose variants with World War 2 combat time on their airframes. The white-trimmed Invaders in the back two rows are from the 8th BS, and those with red fin tips and propeller hubs belong to the 13th BS. The wing was in no fit state to go to war when this shot was taken, being undermanned and well below its full complement of aircraft (Rhodes Elam)*

In June 1950 there were only two understrength squadrons of World War 2-vintage B-26s in the Far East. According to figures held in Fifth Air Force records, the number of flyable Invaders totalled just 26.

Up until late June, there had been no need for alarm, as the Far East was peaceful and the USAF's build up to its goal of an 'all-jet' force was progressing on time. Gone from the inventory were the F-51 Mustangs, leaving only a small fighter force of F-82 Twin Mustangs and B-26s as the last piston-engined types awaiting replacement.

When the North Korean forces breached the 38th Parallel on 25 June, there was instant confusion and a lack of accurate intelligence. Neither the Fifth Air Force or American occupation troops in South Korea were in any fit state to go to war, and the communists were banking on ejecting them before the US war machine could be

placed on a full war footing. North Korean military leaders realised that their invasion had to be decisive, for if the Americans were given the chance to build up their strength in-theatre, their attempts to seize the whole Korean peninsula would be doomed to failure. And that is exactly what happened.

Despite spectacular results in the first weeks of the war, communist forces were soon slowed in their advance by ever-increasing numbers of UN troops, supported by more and more aircraft. Soon, the North Koreans were in full retreat, and it appeared that the war would be won by the Americans, and their allies, 'before Christmas'.

However, in November, neighbouring communist China unexpectedly entered the fray, and over a million Red Army troops pushed UN forces southward in head-long retreat. In an effort to support the advancing

Chinese troops, the communists chose to transport their supplies by truck convoy at night. Only one aircraft was equipped to deal with these nocturnal movements – the Douglas B-26 Invader. By the time the war had ended, units equipped with the Invader had flown almost 54,000 sorties, with at least 42,000 of these taking place at night.

Just three groups would fly the bomber version in Korea, and there were never more than two in-theatre at any one time. The 3rd BW saw action throughout the war, whilst the reserve-manned 452nd BG completed a frontline tour and was then replaced by the 17th BW.

The 3rd BW was initially led into action by Col Virgil L Zoller, whose comments reveal just what his wing went through during those critical early days. His organisation was one squadron short of a full complement, and his allocated flying hours had been severely cut back in the months immediately prior to war erupting. This meant that his flightcrews were ill-prepared for action;

'We had the only aircraft in-theatre capable of flying from a base in Japan with a significant bomb load and hitting targets all over Korea. Our operations improved drastically, even though we had a high loss rate due to operational error. I had my share of these, bouncing high off the ground on landing and coming in with telephone wires wound around the prop hubs. I was very lucky!

'We had a high mission rate brought on by the fact that we were at Iwakuni AB, which put us within easy striking range of most targets. We would fly a mission out of Iwakuni, recover at Taegu, refuel and rearm, and then go do it again. There were some nights when each aircrew

was getting three turnarounds, before they recovered in Japan. When we moved all the way up to Kunsan AB, multiple missions were standard. That's why the tour became 50 missions.

'During those first few missions, we sure needed full support from Fifth AF. This included more aircraft, parts and more aircrews to be rotated in to give our original guys some relief. Well, I was fortunate enough to be able to fly General Partridge on a night mission. He was in the right seat while we were working at a very low altitude under the C-47 flare ships. He enjoyed the mission and liked what he saw. From that time on, we had his full support on what we needed.'

The first time UN air power was really felt by the North Koreans was on the afternoon of 29 June. The war was already four days old, but politics had slowed the USAF's reaction to the invasion. Indeed, it had taken 72 hours to obtain permission to cross the 38th Parallel into North Korea, and when the 'okay' finally came, bad weather in the target area delayed the mission.

At last, at 1615 hours on the afternoon of the 29th, 18 fully-loaded B-26s from the 3rd BW took off from Ashiya. They were hoping to catch an unsuspecting North Korean Peoples' Air Force on the ground at Pyongyang Main Airfield. The timing was intentional, as they wanted to be over the target at dusk.

Most of their load consisted of 'frag' bombs that would be dropped on all of the buildings, hangers and parking areas. If they retained the element of surprise, the B-26s would catch all the enemy aircraft on the ground.

ABOVE The 3rd BW was the first B-26 outfit to see action during the Korean War, and it entered combat with just two understrength squadrons – the 8th and 13th BSs. Amongst the 30-odd B-26s the wing had on strength at the time were these 13th BS B-26Cs, photographed sitting out in the open at Taegu AB in the early autumn of 1950. By this stage of the conflict the frontline had moved far to the north, and the North Korean Army was in full retreat (Harry Galpin)

A good frontal view of the 'business end' of a B-26B, showing its eight forward-firing machine guns mounted in its solid nose fairing. This aircraft was assigned to the 729th BS/452nd BW, and was photographed in early 1951 following the wing's move from Japan to Pusan East (K-9). The reserve-manned 452nd had arrived in Japan in mid-October 1950, and had flown its first missions over Korea on the 27th of the month (Ray Marzullo)

The plan worked to perfection, and UN Intelligence later estimated that 25 aircraft were destroyed on the ground. Only one fighter was able to get airborne, although gunners from one of the B-26s suceeded in fending off the communist aircraft.

Details of this first major bombing mission into North Korea are recalled here by 13th BS Navigator/ Bombardier, Lt Hammond H Bittman;

'We could not fly on the 25th, 26th or 27th due to bad weather. The 28th was also nasty, but clear on top of heavy clouds. It was clear enough above the 32nd Parallel to see the ground. We spotted a train going south and proceeded to drop some 500-lb bombs in front and behind it. Once we had it stopped, we strafed up and down its length. On the second pass we were slammed with heavy machine gun fire that knocked out one of our engines. We limped back to the closest base, which was Suwon. We were relieved to be greeted by American military officers, as there was a possibility that this base had been overrun. There was mass confusion every-where. We managed to get back to our base at Iwakuni.

'Upon arriving back, I was unshaven, tired and needing a bath. It was at that time I discovered that I was to fly lead aircraft for the squadron's first mission over Pyongyang. I could not believe it! But, that is how short we were of flying personnel. There had been a Reduction in force (RIF) a few months before the war started. In many cases, the aircrews had to help refuel the aircraft and load ordnance.

'Anyway, we got our aircraft up there and took out numerous buildings and a few other targets. The early crews got in their missions fast because we were not allowed to get much rest in between. I finished my 50 missions in early August and was reassigned. You would have to have been there during those first few weeks to realise just how hectic things were! The closest call I can remember was with one of our own B-26s over the bomb line. We were headed into North Korea and were talking to the B-26 pilot that we were relieving. As an afterthought, I asked him what his location and altitude was. Before he could answer, he whizzed by us at our exact altitude! We could see the flame from his exhaust as he passed us in the night. To say we puckered up pretty tight would be an understatement!'

Throughout August and the first half of September, B-26 crews faced more pressure than they would at any other point in the Korean War. With communist troops tightening the 'noose' known as the Pusan Perimeter around the embattled UN forces, only the 3rd BW had the capacity to fight back 24 hours a day.

F-80s, F-51s, Corsairs, Panthers and Skyraiders were trying to stem the enemy tide during daylight, but it did not take long for the North Koreans to realise that they could move most of their troops and equipment at night without fear of attack. Up until this time, the two B-26 bomb squadrons (Light) had not conducted night attack operations, so this challenge proved new to them. By Labor Day 1950, the only thing stopping Korea from falling into communist hands was UN air power.

Although the two B-26 wings were having to operate from Japanese bases, they still roamed all over North Korea in search of moving targets. But not all of their ordnance was spent on trucks or trains. They were also in a perfect position to fly harassment missions over enemy positions just as the Po-2 biplane 'hecklers' were doing over air bases in the south. These sorties would disrupt valuable rest time for troops and slow down the movement of supplies. Pilot Lt John R Auer of the 13th BS recalls one of his nights over Pyongyang early in the war;

'I was scheduled to fly a Constant Air Patrol mission over the North Korean capital. On these missions, we were supposed to stay in the vicinity of the city for at least an hour, making periodic passes and firing at anything that moved, or had lights.

'The idea was to disrupt any truck traffic which was operating through the area, which was a major road hub. The tactics to be used were left up to the crew. Some liked to stay at altitude and pickle off a bomb or rocket every few minutes. Since the city was defended by radar-controlled guns, I always preferred to make my passes on the deck, constantly varying my approach direction. This gave me the element of surprise, and I don't believe I was ever even fired at, except perhaps by some small arms. At any rate, I was never hit. My navigator this particular night was known as a "tiger". He used to carry an automatic rifle with him, which he would fire through a port in the nose when the pilot was strafing. I believe he had some kind of death wish!

'Well, on this night, when we arrived in the general vicinity of Pyongyang, it was covered by clouds up to about 10,000 ft. The usual approach when this happened was to dump the load and go home. Since navigation was strictly by dead reckoning, it was a very inexact method of bombing to say the least! At this point, the navigator

BELOW *A formation of 730th BS B-26s returns to base following a ground support mission over the frozen Chosin Reservoir area. This photograph was taken in late 1950, when the weather was unpredictable at best, and usually bad – note that these Invaders are flying over a solid undercast. All three 452nd BW squadrons often had to contend with poor weather during this period, as they regularly flew from Miho AB to targets located in the extreme northern areas of the Korean Peninsula (Myron Brown)*

RIGHT *A nostalgic view of life in the FEAF during the brief period of peace that lasted from September 1945 through to June 1950. Photographed sharing ramp space on the Iwakuni AB flightline in the late spring of 1950 are a Ford Convertible (almost certainly a 1949 model) and the 5th Chadwick. This B-26B had seen action in World War 2, and was just one in a series of Invaders that bore this nickname – all of which were flown by the CO of the 13th BS (Rhodes Elam)*

suggested flying west out over the sea to see if we could find a hole to descend through. That was okay with me, so we flew long enough to be sure we were over water, but found no hole. He then suggested letting down through the cloud to see if we could find the bottom. We did this, and when we reached 1000 ft, I levelled off and said it was no use, and that I was climbing back up on top.

'He kept talking and convinced me to drop down to 500 ft, at which point we broke out. It was so dark that I had to continue to fly on instruments. We flew due east to see if we could spot the coastline. He was flying in the nose where it was completely dark, and he spotted the breakers on the beach. I could see nothing, but was adjusted to the dimly lit instrument panel.

'We figured we were north of Pyongyang, so we flew south along the coast, trying to find the river that would lead us straight to the city. A short time later, he was able to see the river and still I could see nothing! He talked me along the river and between the mountains until I finally saw some lights ahead. The weather was so nasty that I pickled off all of my ordnance as we made one high-speed pass over the target. With the run completed, I climbed up on top and headed home. The navigator got to fire his rifle as we made the low pass over Pyongyang.'

Nocturnal targets were always in abundance, as senior 13th BS Invader pilot Lt Charles Bartels recounts;

'It was the first day of September, and we were directed to an area that was close to the Han River. The US 25th Infantry Division was taking a lot of "heat" from the NKPA. When we arrived overhead, an Army ground control unit marked the target area with a few rounds of white phosphorous. I manoeuvred my hard-nose gunship into a position from where I would attack on an east to west heading, laying down a string of 100-lb General Purpose (GP) bombs. These were released at specific intervals, so I could cover the entire column of enemy troops. Finishing this run, I banked sharply, lining up for a firing pass with my 14 forward-firing 0.5-in guns.

'I continued this routine until I had run out of ammunition. In my bomb flashes I saw nothing but masses of troops, and they were catching the brunt of my attack. My controller evidently knew they were forming up for a human wave attack against his division because he directed me right into the middle of them. Our attacks in this area prevented heavy casualties from being inflicted on US troops, and it saved the high ground they were trying to hold. I heard that the body count taken the next morning was staggering.'

BELOW The winter of 1950-51 left most Americans in no doubt as to just how bitterly cold the weather could be in the Far East. Things might have slowed down due to several feet of snow, but operations never came to a halt. With the B-26s grounded due to the inclement winter weather, these enlisted troops have taken time out to ski behind a jeep. The key to a successful run was to ensure that the driver steered a steady course between the parked aeroplanes! These B-26s belong to the 729th BS, and are sat on the ramp at Miho (Robert Hansen)

The 'fist' that was tightening the grip on the 'perimeter' was finally cut off when the US Marines performed an audacious amphibious landing at Inchon, in North Korea, and moved inland to sever the enemy's supply routes. At the same time that news of the invasion reached North Korean troops entrenched above Pusan, a major breakout offensive by UN forces commenced.

The co-ordination between the two actions was well timed, and the enemy broke and ran, the thought of being completely cut off from friendly territory playing heavily on the minds of most communist troops. Now the situation had gone from gradual retreat to headlong invasion, with UN forces advancing northward. Many North Koreans believed General Douglas MacArthur would stop there, but his goal was the entire Korean Peninsula!

By then, the wheels had already been put in motion to bring in one of the largest B-26 wings from the USA. The 452nd BW was a reserve-manned organisation based at Long Beach, California, and was comprised of four squadrons – the 728th, 729th, 730th and 731st BSs. There was a reason for bringing a four-squadron wing over. As previously mentioned, the 3rd BW had been operating with only two units since the start of hostilities, and needed a third squadron to make it an effective

combat wing. The 731st would therefore be attached to the 3rd once the 452nd arrived in-theatre. The new wing flew into Itazuke AB in October 1950, and on the 27th of that month flew its first official combat mission – exactly 77 days after the reservists had been activated. The wing's main base, in the interim, would be at Miho, in Japan.

The 731st BS was the first squadron within the 452nd to depart for the Far East, leaving Victorville, California, on 15 October, en route to McClellan Field. Once there, it broke up into four-ship flights, with each being assigned to a B-29 'mother-ship'. The most memorable of the legs on the long flight was the one from California to Hickam Field, Hawaii, which took ten hours. The next day the unit flew to Johnston Island, then to Kwajalein and Guam. The transpac finally ended when the bombers landed at Tachikawa, on the outskirts of Tokyo.

Within a few days the squadron was ready for combat, and it would soon make the night interdiction role its own – so much so that all 731st BS aircraft were painted black overall.

During the first six months of the Korean War the fortunes of either side waxed and waned. There was the sudden communist push southward almost as far as the southern tip of Korea. This was followed by the UN thrust

northwards to the North Korean-Chinese border. And finally, the same UN forces rapidly retreated back to below the 38th Parallel when attacked by the numerically superior Chinese Red Army.

Prior to China's intervention, activity had slowed in Korea itself by the late autumn of 1950. The North Koreans were jammed into a small pocket backed up against Manchuria, and they posed very little threat. This in turn meant that the patrol sectors for the B-26s had shrunk. However, in those areas where the enemy was still well organised, truck activity associated with the re-supply effort continued to be targeted. Strategically, all industrial targets along the Yalu River had been destroyed by B-29s, and to many the war seemed to be almost over.

On the night of 2 November 1950, the 8th Cavalry Regiment 'locked up' with the Chinese Army near Unsan. Although the new enemy force had been probing RoK lines for several days, this was the first encounter between Chinese and American ground forces. The waning war had just been rejuvenated through the input of literally hundreds of thousands of fresh Chinese troops. The fighting that had seemed to be all but over would now continue for another 32 months! The air war had only just begun.

The total number of B-26 bomb squadrons to see combat during the remaining 31 months of war totalled just six – effectively two wings. An RB-26 squadron also operated out of Kimpo as part of the 67th Tactical Reconnaissance Wing, although its primary weapons were cameras rather than bombs.

Once the Chinese Army had established a geographical base within Korea, its logistics train moved in and started the re-supply mission. Despite, facing aggressive fighter-bombers during the day and B-26 bombers and Marine fighter-bombers at night, the Chinese still managed to keep supplies flowing south .

North Korea had no straight super highways running north/south at this time. Being a very mountainous country, its primary transport routes were a network of roads that ran in every direction, joined by a complex system of interconnections. This meant that no single bomb could shut the road system down, and instead it was left to the B-26 units to slow things up.

Daylight missions at low altitudes proved to be extremely dangerous, as 728th BS pilot Capt Charles Kamanski (on his tenth combat mission) relates;

'We were leading a strike against Sariwon, a town west of Pyongyang. Our orders were to hit anything

ABOVE *The 452nd BW hit the ground running when it entered the Korean War. They had to fly long missions out of Miho, and most sorties at that time were still taking place during the hours of daylight. This meant that many of its aircraft suffered varying degress of battle damage at the hands of North Korean radar-guided flak batteries, not to mention small arms fire. One such victim was this B-26B, which crash-landed at Taegu AB in the autumn of 1950. Having been shot up over the target, and had its right engine knocked out, the Invader's right main gear leg gave way upon landing. This photograph was taken by a 4th Fighter Wing pilot who was flying F-86s out of Taegu at the time (Jack Wingo)*

INSET *The ground fire thrown up by Chinese truck convoys was often deadly accurate, and invariably intense. Fortunately, the ruggedly-built B-26 usually made it back to base and lived to fight again – as was the case with this 452nd BG bomber. The concentrated flak damage was inflicted on the night of 15 May 1951 as the Invader pulled up from its strafing run (Robert Stoner)*

MAIN PICTURE *This 729th BS B-26 has just been loaded with 500-lb bombs at Pusan East in 1951, the truck which delivered the ordnance being driven off in the direction of the next aircraft on the flightline. The impending night mission called for a maximum load-out of GP bombs, which meant weapons secured both internally and under the wings. Such ordnance was typically used to inflict as many rail cuts as was possible with a single aircraft. This photograph was taken soon after the 452nd BG had moved to Korea from Japan (Ken Lamoreux)*

moving south of the bomb line. After my initial pass, I spotted a locomotive pulling several cars, which seemed to be undamaged. The cold weather had set in, as this was soon after the Chinese had entered the war, and things were not going well. As I lined up for my pass, I noticed a lot of troops in an open field between me and the engine. I fired a couple of high velocity aerial rockets (5-in HVARs) at the locomotive, and at the same time I was raking my machine gun fire all over the troops.

'I noticed that they were taking refuge behind what appeared to be kilns that were in a brick yard. I was coming in on the engine and cars at tree-top level. Suddenly, one of the kilns exploded, sending thousands of bricks into the air. There was no time to react! I flew into the debris and it was like getting hit with a baseball bat! I was knocked unconscious, and came to on the crosswind leg of a left hand racetrack pattern. I looked up and there was a hole in the windscreen, and I was covered with blood and pieces of brick!

'The moment that I was hit, I slumped over the controls. My navigator, Lt Marvin Jackson, pulled me back and was able to take over. He got us back up to about 100 ft and turned the bomber into the crosswind leg. We couldn't have been more than 50 ft off the ground when we hit the bricks. I can remember my gunner, Sgt Taylor, calling out that the leading edges of our horizontal and vertical stabilisers had been flattened by the bricks. Fortunately, everything was working okay, so I decided to make another pass on the enemy troops.

'We expended all of our ordnance and were able to make it back to the closest friendly base, which at the time was Pyongyang. As I was loaded into a C-54 for the flight back to Japan, I could hear the artillery fire in the distance. We were about to be kicked out of that area. I

lost the sight in my left eye as a result of the explosion, but was able to continue flying combat in the Invader. I finished my tour with 55 missions.'

Most of the press releases issued by the Fifth Air Force on the nocturnal forays of its B-26 Invaders pertained to the two bomb wings that were fighting the war every night with three squadrons apiece.

However, there was an additional unit that was rarely mentioned, this unique outfit keeping a low profile. Flying glass-nosed RB-26Cs, the 12th Tactical Reconnaissance Squadron (Night Photo) performed the crucial task of intelligence gathering at a time when UN forces were in dire need of any type of information on what the enemy was getting up to during the hours of darkness.

To satisfy this demand, the unit (then designated the 162nd Tactical Reconnaissance Squadron) had been hastily sent to Japan in August 1950. Once assigned its combat role, the squadron had become the 12th TRS.

The importance of its mission increased rapidly as the Chinese and North Korean armies stepped up their nocturnal re-supply efforts. Initially, the 12th operated simultaneously from both Komaki and Tsuiki ABs, in Japan. However, once the frontline had stabilised in the spring of 1951, the squadron moved up to Kimpo AB (K-14), where it remained until the war had ended.

The RB-26Cs of the 12th TRS became a vital part of the 67th Tactical Reconnaissance Wing (TRW), the converted bombers being just one of four dedicated reconnaissance types flown by the wing during its lengthy tour of duty in Korea. The Invader unit had a simple mission brief – keep enemy airfields, supply dumps, railroads and supply routes under constant surveillance at night. This information was in turn relayed back to the FEAF, and in a lot of cases it would trigger the hasty despatch of a strike package which invariably included examples of the bomber variant of the venerable B-26.

BELOW *The early months of 1951 were witness to much activity in and around Seoul City Airport (K-16), which became a military airfield due to a number of the future main USAF bases not yet being fully operational following their initial abandonment in the face of the Chinese offensive. This photograph shows an unidentified B-26 (either a 13th or 729th BS machine) and two Marine F4U Corsairs parked outside the shell of large hangar. K-16 also served as the forward base for at least one F-51 squadron (Max Tomich)*

INSET LEFT *A 729th BS Invader warms up before taxying away from the squadron ramp at Pusan East AB in 1951. Five weeks after the Korean War had started, the 452nd BW was activated for combat, and it brought all four of its squadrons (including the 729th BS) to Japan to support the 3rd BW (Ken Lamoreux)*

INSET RIGHT *In May 1951 the 452nd moved its aircraft from Miho to Pusan East, where the wing would remain for the remainder of its tour. This photograph was taken soon after the move, and its shows a squadron-strength daylight strike being formed up on the various taxyways. Aircraft of the 728th BS (green-marked) have already begun their take-off runs, while the 729th (red) have completed their engine starts and are ready to roll. The 452nd BW was heavily involved in the day mission tasking throughout this period (Ken Lamoreaux)*

MAIN PICTURE *During the first year of the war extra precautions were taken to protect aircraft from surprise attacks at night. Such camouflaging proved very effective, for only a few North Korean Po-2 biplane types succeeded in causing damage to equipment, and the nocturnal raiders were soon stopped by American nightfighters. Seen at Taegu in early 1951, the aircraft in the foreground is a 27th Fighter-Bomber Wing F-84 Thunderjet, whilst the B-26 behind it belongs to the 452nd BW (Guy Brown)*

RIGHT *An element of 729th BS Invaders are seen striking at a North Korean village which almost certainly housed hundreds of labourers that worked each night to repair the rail lines shown at the far right. Trains could be running on a repaired line within hours of it suffering major damage thanks to the skill of the repair teams. By 'taking out' these key personnel, the rail lines remained inoperable for longer. This mission was the most dangerous allocated to B-26 crews during daylight hours, for it required the target to be hit with precision from very low level (Guy Brown)*

BELOW RIGHT *Capt Myron Brown was one of the original cadre of 730th BS pilots posted to Korea in October 1950, and he is seen here posing in front of his hard-nose gunship at Miho AB. The 452nd would officially end its tour in Korea on 10 May 1952, when they were inactivated and the 17th BW immediately formed in its place. This swapping of wings was essentially little more than an administrative paper change, for the aircraft flown by the 17th from Pusan East had been previously assigned to the 452nd. Indeed, the only real change was that the Invaders now boasted different squadron colours (Myron Brown)*

LEFT *A lone RB-26C from the 12th TRS taxies out at the start of yet another mission over North Korea. As the nocturnal 'eyes and ears' of the FEAF, these nightflying RB-26s sought out any potential communist targets during the hours of darkness. In-theatre through to the end of the conflict, the 12th had the honour of flying the very last combat sortie of the Korean War (George Ballweg)*

BELOW *A 12th TRS 'Blackbird' returns from a pre-dawn mission over enemy territory. Despite flying in a combat zone from a forward operating area, the unit enjoyed one of best safety records of any squadron in the USAF, completing 10,000 operational hours without experiencing a single major accident. The 12th TRS was one of three units assigned to the 67th TRW (Alva Wilkerson)*

ABOVE On 19 June 1951 the 3rd BW's 731st BS flew its 10,000th combat sortie. Much was made of this operational milestone, and the flightline at Iwakuni AB was the location selected as the venue for the FEAF's celebration of this feat. This photograph was taken just hours after the sortie had been flown. Note the Royal Australian Air Force (RAAF) C-47s, Meteors and Mustangs lined up behind the suitably decorated B-26. Iwakuni was one of the RAAF's primary facilities in the Far East, the Australians having had aircraft based there since the end of World War 2 (David Wilson)

ABOVE LEFT *Lt Ray Marzullo's Invader awaits the arrival of its crew at Pusan East in June 1951. By then the bad weather of the previous winter had eased up, and all six B-26 squadrons had their hands full attacking communist targets – the Chinese were pouring supplies down all road and rail routes under the cover of darkness. Lt Marzullo was responsible for a spectacular ammunition train kill at dusk which resulted in secondary explosions continuing for at least 12 hours after the initial attack (Ray Marzullo)*

LEFT *Freshly painted and fully bombed up, 8th BS B-26C THE BIG "O"/THE TERRIBLE SWEDE was photographed at Kunsan AB (K-8) soon after the squadron had tranferred in from Japan on 18 August 1951. Led at the time by Lt Col Stanley V Rush, the 8th would remain at K-8 until the war ended in July 1953 (Ray Anastos)*

ABOVE *During the summer months at Pusan East the surrounding scenery could be outstanding. Bombed up with a full load of ordnance, there was only one way to take off from the base in a B-26, and that was out to sea. The remaining three air corridors were all surrounded by mountains, and to make matters worse, the take-off route took the Invaders over a veritable armada of unloaded ammunition ships anchored in the nearby bay! These sun-drenched Invaders were assigned to the 730th BS (Bob Schultz)*

RIGHT *Not all Invader missions ended on a happy note! This 452nd BW B-26 flew its assigned sector and expended all of its ordnance on road traffic, but was badly shot up by flak in the process. After limping back to the closest friendly base, it crashed on landing. What little debris remained of the bomber has been pushed off to the side of the runway (Ray Marzullo)*

CHAPTER TWO

TRUCK AND TRAIN BUSTING

The entry of China into the Korean War was perfectly timed. The communist superpower could have sent its vast army into North Korea once UN forces crossed the 38th Parallel, but it chose to wait. Once the first snows began to fall and the weather turned inclement, the Chinese automatically enjoyed the element of surprise.

The US intelligence service had long believed that the Chinese would enter the conflict should the North Korean offensive become bogged down. After all, this was a political war, and one communist regime would surely back another in the fight against the capitalist West.

However, the final word on the Chinese threat came from the office of the supreme UN commander in-

theatre, Gen Douglas MacArthur, and he and his people proclaimed that 'the Chinese will not cross the Yalu'.

In the days leading up to the surprise attack, B-26 crews reported much activity across the river at night, these sightings being supported by the Marine F4U-5N nightfighter squadron VMF(N)-513. The reports went straight to MacArthur, who dismissed them as nothing to worry about. How wrong history proved him to be.

By New Year's Day 1951, the Chinese had pushed so far south that they had begun to mass thousands of trucks on the Manchurian border in an effort to improve the flow of supplies to their advancing troops. With hundreds of thousands of fighting men constantly on the move,

BELOW *These B-26Cs (one from both the 8th and 13th BSs) prepare to start their engines and move over to the main runway at Taegu AB in early 1952. Both aircraft were working the same 'shift', but in a different sector (Don Baker)*

logistical support was crucial to the success of the offensive. And despite increased UN airpower in-theatre, the Chinese seemed to be able to keep their troops supplied with the minimum of effort.

Marauding fighter-bombers found little movement during the day amongst the charred remains of vehicles and rail cars that had been destroyed the previous night. Instead, pilots concentrated on making rail cuts and knocking out buildings, suspected ammunition dumps and truck depots that had been camouflaged.

The B-26 squadrons rated their own performance during this crucial phase in the war by the number of trucks and locomotives they had knocked out. Both targets were strictly nocturnal, and could only be found by picking over dark mountainous terrain. The trains would dart from one tunnel to another, with some open stretches lasting for barely a mile.

The most successful locomotive hunters all seemed to share the same trait – combat experience. This meant that they new which tactics to employ, and the dangers associated with this hazardous mission. The terrain was dangerous and the visibility was always poor, yet Invader

pilots kept descending to tree-top level to hit their quarry night after night. The biggest threat they faced when working along the bottom of the many mountain valleys were the flak guns positioned on the ridges above them.

Lt Walt McGinnis was a pilot with the 34th BS, and he became one of the top-scoring train killers in Korea. Here, he relates some of his experiences;

'Two very memorable missions were flown on the nights of 25 and 26 February 1953. On the first, my take-off time was at 1810 hours. We were pre-briefed to recce from Wonsan, north along the east coast of North Korea. After about 30 miles, I came upon a train five miles south of Kowon, at the exact spot that my crew and I had destroyed a locomotive and 20 boxcars on the night of 31 January. I made an immediate dive-bombing attack and dropped an M-47 firebomb that landed on the locomotive. This stopped the train, and made an excellent marker for further level-bombing runs from a race track pattern.

'My navigator/bombardier, a Lt Spear, put a 500-lb GP bomb right on the engine on one of the subsequent passes. Two more firebombs that I dropped missed the train entirely, probably because we were being harassed

on every pass by two anti-aircraft guns sited on hills on either side of the train. After taking as much of that as I could handle, I strafed and destroyed one of the positions. The other one shut down entirely. We then set the train alight from one end to the other.

'The next night we took off at 2400 hours with the same assigned sector. At Tanchon, we sighted about 20 cars being pulled by one engine. I made the first dive-bomb attack, dropping two 500-lb bombs. The first one hit the locomotive straight on, blowing it up. We then made consecutive attacks to destroy the boxcars it was pulling. We ran into a lot of trouble in the form of a 40 mm anti-aircraft battery positioned up in the hills. He would only shoot when we turned away from him, so I couldn't spot where he was.

'In an effort to get the upper hand, I called in another B-26 to hit the train while I pretended to leave the area, loitering just out of earshot from the gunner. Sure enough, as soon as the other Invader made a pass, the gunner opened up. I pin-pointed his position and went after him with my 0.5-in guns, which chewed both the gun and gunner up. Between the two B-26s, all of the boxcars and engine were destroyed. Some of my missions lasted for six hours on just a regular fuel load. That was a long time to sit in an unheated cockpit where temperatures

were sometimes as low as a -30°C. Of the 50 missions that I flew, 14 were rail-recce types against locomotives.'

A large number of the boxcars being hit were carrying ammunition, which generated spectacular secondary explosions. To a B-26 crew, this equated to a standing ovation for a job well done! The 452nd BW's Lt Ray Marzullo remembers one of his missions that led to a rather lengthy series of explosions;

'When I arrived in Korea as a replacement pilot, the mission had been changed to night operations, with a maximum limit of 55 night combat missions. In addition to night strikes and road recce, SHORAN (SHOrt range RAdar Navigation) bombing was used during inclement weather. The accuracy was remarkable, and since there were precious few of these aircraft, they were often used as pathfinders for other B-26s.

'The most exciting mission I can recall flying was when I destroyed a 27-car ammunition/fuel train on a dusk/night armed reconnaissance mission. The train was emerging from a tunnel, where it had been hiding during daylight hours. Due to the high intensity of ground fire, only one strafing/bomb pass was planned.

'While strafing and dropping fragmentation bombs, the train exploded into one huge fireball! Unable to avoid the explosion, we flew right through it. I was sure I had

ABOVE *Unloading after a 'hard day's night' in the spring of 1952. The only task left for these flightcrews prior to getting some sleep is the debriefing. The proliferation of yellow caps indicates that these men belong to the 8th BS at Kunsan AB. Despite this unit being on manoeuvres at Ashiya AB, in Japan, when the war started, its response to the crisis was almost instantaneous (Hans Petermann)*

ABOVE THE 6TH CHADWICK *was the personal mount of 13th BS boss, Lt Col Robert Fortney. In early 1952, he attacked a column of trucks with rockets, and as he pulled up over the target, one of the vehicles exploded. The resulting damage can be clearly seen here in this post-mission. photograph. The Invader was duly flown to Japan, where it was fitted with a new nose section. Two months later, a young pilot returning from North Korea performed two barrel rolls over the base in the bomber, thus inflicting fatal damage to the wing spars! The Invader was subsequently Class 26'd (written off) (John Thomson)*

done myself in, but the old B-26 was built like a tank. It emerged out the other side of the fireball with no visible damage. I learned later through intelligence and photo recce that the train burned and exploded for about 12 hours! This loss had to hurt the enemy quite a bit!'

There were few long stretches of railway line in North Korea. However, there was one extended segment of track that wound down a long valley just south of the Yalu River. If a B-26 was fortunate enough to catch a train out in the open in this valley, it would not be an easy kill, for an impressive array of anti-aircraft guns had been sited in the surrounding hills. Lt James Becker of the 13th BS recalls a nocturnal foray into this valley;

'We were assigned a lot of missions up on the "purple" routes close to Manchuria, which always saw a lot of activity. On this particular night, however, the hunting was bad. Indeed, it was so poor that we got down extremely low so we wouldn't miss anything.

'We soon saw a train in a long valley that was about to cross a bridge. We flew around it so that we could hit it broadside. On our first pass, we dropped four 260-lb

frags that were a bit long, but a few of them hit the train causing it to come to a halt. The second pass saw us drop the same ordnance, and again they landed a bit short. On the third pass we expended two napalm bombs that also hit the ground short, although the resulting wall of flame flowed up and over the train. Then we flew past the back end of the long line of railcars and strafed its entire length.

'By now, we had alerted every anti-aircraft battery in the valley. It was a withering wall of fire, and we had to get down so low that we were pulling up to go over fences! The flak was all coming from a long ridge of hills west of us. We made it through the gauntlet, but if we had gained about 15-20 ft of altitude, they would have nailed us right there.'

If the above-mentioned mission had been flown in a glass-nose B-26C, one can only imagine the nervous state the crewmen riding 'up front' must have been in upon the aircraft's return to base. Indeed, one pilot described his low-level exploits at night as like being a passenger on 'the roller coaster of death!' Another individual who experinced just such a ride was enlisted crewman Sgt Lee M Adams, who had only recently transferred into the 730th BS;

'My first mission was to fly as an observer in the front of a B-26C named *Neva Hoppen*. The sortie took us up near Sinanju. I had no idea what to expect. We were flying along in the clear bright night sky at about 8000 ft. Most of the sound of the two R2800s was behind us. I was thinking just how great and peaceful this was!

'Suddenly, the whole world lit up! As we came into the target area, the anti-aircraft let loose on us. Of course there is nothing out front of us but angry tracers – millions of them! They were coming so close they actually made a red glow inside the Plexiglas nose. I can still feel how I tried to get away by pushing back against the bulkhead of the compartment. Fortunately, we made it back in one piece.

'I heard of a couple of nose gear failures, back at Pusan East where the guys sitting in the nose section were either killed or badly hurt. The view was spectacular, but the risk made it a gamble!'

On a later mission Sgt Adams courted death yet again when his B-26 attempted to deliver a load of 260-lb frag bombs. He was awarded a Distinguished Flying Cross for this particular sortie;

'I received that award for getting out into the open bomb-bay while over enemy territory (twice). It seems we had a hung up frag bomb, and I was elected to go out and release the device. It was not a matter of being a hero, but if we didn't get the bombs loose, we couldn't land safely. The rear bomb hanger was where the trouble was. The front end of the bomb dropped down, allowing the arming wire to pull free and arm the bomb. I couldn't get out into the bomb bay with my parachute on, so I took it off and slipped out the back entrance of the gunner's compartment.

'With a flashlight in my mouth and a screwdriver in my left hand, I reached out with my right arm and took hold of the only thing I could, which was the manual flap crank, and stepped out onto the edges of the open bomb bay. As the bomb came loose, it hit my foot, tore my glove off, knocked the flashlight out of my mouth and the screwdriver is stuck somewhere in a North Korean mountainside. Somehow, I managed to hold onto the flap handle and get back into the gunner's compartment. My hands still sweat to this day when I think of that mission!'

The 3rd and 17th BWs each boasted three squadrons with histories that dated back to the World War I era. Steeped in tradition, with impressive lineage, both wings were regular Air Force organisations, while

BELOW *This was almost certainly the final* CHADWICK *in the long series of so-named bombers flown by 13th BS commanders, this tradition dating all the way back to the early years of World War 2, when the unit flew the A-20 Havoc. As previously mentioned, the 13th's skipper during* THE SIXTH *and* SEVENTH CHADWICK *era was Lt Col Robert Fortney, who authorised the special red paint scheme applied to this B-26 (Robert Fortney)*

The crew of this hard-nose 13th BS B-26B commence their pre-flight walkaround checks in preparation for the impending night sortie. The bomber has already received its internal load of 500-lb GP bombs, and the magazines for its battery of six 0.5-in machine guns have been fully replenished. Such a deadly combination was usually fatal to any locomotives that were unfortunate enough to be caught out in the open by the marauding B-26 crew. This photograph was taken at Kunsan in late 1952 (Al Keeler)

A mission-weary B-26 crew head for the ever-ready crew shuttle pick-up truck after completing a pre-dawn sortie over one of the 'Purple' routes. The groundcrew have already begun their preparations for turning the aircraft around in time for the next crew, who will fly it out in the late afternoon – provided there is no significant battle damage. The red trim indicates that this B-26 is a 37th BS machine, photographed at Pusan East in the early autumn of 1952 (Dan Paveo)

RIGHT *Examples of the specialised loading equipment ordnance types depended on in Korea can be seen in this photograph of a 34th BS B-26. In the foreground is a modified GMC truck, which boasts a sturdy wrought iron A-frame and winching rail for loading and unloading all manner of ordnance from HVARs to 1000-lb GP bombs. Behind the truck, recently delivered 500-lb GP bombs are being jacked up into place beneath the wing pylons, before being secured to the mountings. The mountains in the background bracketed Pusan East on three sides, which meant that heavily-laden B-26s had to take-off in the direction of the harbour (Don Wickler)*

the 452nd was reserve-manned. Each unit sported a large sign in front of its operations shack, which proudly listed the campaigns and battles that the squadron had been involved in. Of all the B-26 units in Korea, the 13th BS undoubtedly had one of the most unique traditions, which dated back to the early days of World War 2.

The 13th was then equipped with an earlier example of the Douglas medium bomber in the form of the A-20 Havoc, and the tradition evolved whereby the squadron commander flew an aircraft decorated both with a distinctive marking and nickname. At that time the unit's call sign was 'Chadwick', and this soon appeared on the nose of the CO's A-20, along with a wheel marking painted on both sides of the vertical stabiliser. So started the famous 'Chadwick' series of aircraft, and by the time the Korean War commenced, the squadron was onto its fifth 'Chadwick'. A further two so-named B-26s saw action during the conflict, with the seventh 'Chadwick' being flown through to the July 1953 truce by the 13th BS's final wartime CO, Lt Col Robert Fortney.

It was the sixth 'Chadwick' that truly made a name for itself, being used by numerous pilots other than Fortney, who recalls;

'Old No 6 – I really don't know exactly what to say about my affair with the "6th Chadwick". It had the tail code "Y", with six 0.5-in machine guns in the nose. Shortly after I took command of the 13th, I had the nose and the forward half of the fuselage back to the bomb-bay painted red to really show off our squadron's colours. One night in February 1952 I had a mission for which I was armed with either six or eight 5-in HVARs in addition to the normal bomb load and ammo for the guns.

'I don't remember the exact route we were covering, but we were nearly finished and I still had not shot all of my rockets. We spotted a line of vehicles moving down a road and I immediately lined up for a pass. The terrain around there was fairly flat, so I figured I could get right in on them at a low altitude.

'Those rockets, even though they were mounted under the wings, gave off a bright glare when they were

LEFT *The 90th BS could boast the 'top timer' B-26 in-theatre, as the mission log on this aircraft clearly shows! The Invader's frontline career came to a tragic end soon after this photograph was taken (by an F-84 pilot who also flew out of Kunsan AB) when it crashed on a routine flight to Japan (Harold Beasley)*

fired in pitch darkness, which would tend to temporarily blind the pilot. As you can imagine, when they hit and exploded, debris flew up in the air. As it turned out, I was so low that I flew into the debris, which included a lot of mud. That caused several holes to be punctured in the nose, and splattered a considerable amount of mud on the windscreen. Something also hit a control rod for the prop on the right engine. I was no longer able to control the pitch of the prop, but it was set so that I could continue to fly the bomber without having to feather it.

'We made it safely back to Kunsan, and after the nose section was repaired, the aircraft was put right back in the rotation. It wasn't long after this that one of my pilots barrel rolled it once or twice when he arrived back over the base! He accomplished his manoeuvres, but warped the wings so badly in the process that the entire aircraft was Class 26'd (written off). The replacement aircraft also got a bright red paint job, and it became the seventh "Chadwick". It was No 698, which had a solid nose with eight 0.5-in machine guns in it. If I remember correctly, it had the letter "R" on the tail.'

High-velocity rockets had been widely used on fighter types during the closing months of World War 2, and these had evolved into a very lethal weapon by the late summer of 1945. The 5-in HVARs were officially tested on the A-26 Invader in late 1945 by the 89th BS (which, at the time, was part of the 3rd BW). It duly published a detailed report, which can be summarized as follows;

'All the rockets were found to have an effective range, with a flat trajectory, of 4000 yards. The exact range of the rocket varied because of the wide gap of burn time from the rocket motor. The most effective method of firing was found to be from an altitude of approximately 750 ft at 350 mph in a shallow dive at a range of 3500 yards.'

The only negative aspect to come out of these tests was the minimum altitude at which the rockets had to be fired, for in the event of a huge secondary explosion, the attacking Invader would shoot itself down. The report also determined that the average pilot would have to fire at least 28 rockets before he could achieve a good degree of accuracy. Bear in mind that none of the testing was conducted at night, which proved to be the arena in which the B-26 would be required to fight.

With clear moonlit nights proving the exception rather than the norm over Korea, B-26 crews often had to rely upon flares in order to get down to tree-top level. When properly placed by the C-47 'Firefly' unit that operated out of Taegu and Kimpo, the Invader crews could effectively cover a significant length of road. Using the call sign 'Lamplighter', the specially-rigged C-47s stayed on station for a very a long time, and proved critical in securing successful runs over the deadly 'Purple' routes.

Lt Donald Soefker, a pilot in the 'Grim Reaper' squadron, recounts some of his more memorable missions where he depended on flares;

BELOW Support personnel for the 90th BS waste no time in getting their Invaders ready for the impending night missions. The fuel truck in the background and the bomb truck to the right of the photograph supplied the endurance and punch for a successful night of hunting over the roads and railway lines of North Korea. The 90th BS was the third squadron within the 3rd BW, its aircraft being easily identified by the white trim worn on the vertical stabiliser (Walter Zust)

'Most, if not all of my missions were along the west coast. I spent a lot of time in "Purple-13", which was from Sinuiju, on the Yalu River, down to Sinanju – a very dangerous place to be at any time! Most nights it was very dark, and we didn't get much help from the moon. I would call for "Lamplighter" and tell him my destination. They would be there, overhead, and ready for my instructions. Of course there were some areas that were out of his reach, like "Purple-13". First, I'd have them drop a flare and I would give them the corrections for the next one. When we had it right, he would drop a string of flares that would light up the entire route for some distance.

'My gunner, Sgt Al Roth, would always go down the flightline and load us up with flares in case we were working beyond any of the flare ships' range. How he was able to drop them out of the aircraft I'll never know. I just opened the bomb bay doors and he'd get them out. One night we were working the route north of Sariwon. Trucks were moving like ants to the south toward the village. Of course, they would shut off their headlights when a spotter signalled that an aircraft was in the vicinity. I contacted "Lamplighter" and he said they could also see the trucks, so I had him set out a string of flares right down the highway.

'We were flying north to south. It was almost like working during the day. I immediately went down to about 50 ft with all 14 forward-firing '50s blazing. Gunner Roth was having a field day firing his lower turret to the rear. Neither one of us could miss at that distance. Suddenly, the sky lit up over us with red fire from the flak positions that were on either side of us. It formed a canopy of imminent death, so I decided to continue at that low altitude. To have pulled up would have been suicidal!

'You might wonder why they didn't shoot us down at such close range? I could see the sandbagged gun positions on either side of the road. "Lamplighter" had the area lit up like daytime. The answer to this question was that they could not depress their guns any further due to the sandbagging.

'I guess they were as frustrated as I was grateful! There was one mission where I was so low that I hit the top of a tree that I was sure I could clear. It was on the outskirts of a village I was attacking. Most of the aggressive pilots flew this low on numerous occasions as that is what it took to get the job done, and to survive. Your concentration is so great that the low altitude doesn't really bother you as much as you would think.'

ABOVE *The large bomb dump at Pusan East was well protected against a sneak air attack, being quite a distance from the flightline, and heavily reveted with sandbags. However, the most dangerous threat came from sabotage, and not nocturnal attack from the air. The General Purpose bombs shown here are a mix of 500- and 1000-lb weapons. On most missions, B-26s had to haul this ordnance the entire length of the Korean Peninsula in order to reach designated targets (Will Plentl)*

MAIN PICTURE *Although this B-26 has been loaded with the required ordnance, the maintenance crews have evidently encountered an engine problem that is taking longer than anticipated to rectify. The large brown drop tank inboard of the HVARs is filled with napalm, which was the most feared weapon used by any UN aircraft in Korea. In interviews conducted by journalists long after the war, Chinese war veterans that were living in the Hong Kong area stated that if they were caught above ground by this deadly petroleum-based incendiary, it would cling on and burn right through any clothing they were wearing (Ken Lamoreux)*

INSET *A 13th BS B-26C arrives back from a spell at the FEAF's rear echelon maintenance facility in Japan. During daylight hours, most 3rd BW Invaders would be parked on the ramp, undergoing preparation for that night's series of missions. This gave budding photographers within the wing plenty of opportunity to record the various aircraft on film (Albert Emanuel)*

With the trucks' running lights dimmed, and no flares to illuminate the target area, it was almost impossible to spot the convoys. In these situations, B-26 crews often resorted to playing a 'cat-and-mouse' game with the truck drivers. Flying at high altitude, surveying a wide area of terrain, pilots scoured the night sky for moving lights on the roads below them, striving to pin-point the trucks' location.

Sgt Chet Leroy, a gunner with the 90th BS, relates a memorable mission that resulted in a single truck being destroyed without any ordnance being expended;

'It was standard procedure to turn off the navigation lights when passing over "Oboe", inbound to the target area. "Oboe" was the name of an island check-point just off the coast of Korea.

'On this particular night I was right seat engineer, and the pilot and I noticed that the flak was heavier and closer than usual, but not close enough to worry about. When then made a head-on strafing run on a truck, but before we could fire our guns, the truck's headlights started going in an erratic pattern and one light suddenly went out. We pulled up, somewhat puzzled.

'Since we didn't draw any flak from the area, we started another dive on the truck, but this time we extended the landing lights! The truck was part way down an embankment, wrecked. We spent the rest of the night's mission inadvertently decreasing their rice output, which is another way of saying that some of our ordnance exploded in the rice paddies instead of damaging trucks. There just wasn't anything out there, or at least it seemed that way to us.

'On the way out of our patrol area, we passed by "Oboe" again. At that time, I reached up to the centre overhead panel to turn on the navigation lights, only to discover that we had never turned them off when we came into our target area! This explained the better than normal flak accuracy, and the incident with the single truck. The driver had seen our lights as we dived in on him, and he probably bailed out of the truck, which sent it rolling down an embankment. So, we destroyed one truck with no ammo or ordnance spent.

'There was also the possibility that our lights had been spotted far off, and any trucks moving in the area immediately shut their lights off and came to a stop. They saw us and we never saw them!'

Although the night intruder role was a favourite amongst B-26 crews, it wasn't the only mission that they flew. Every one of the six Invader squadrons involved in

LEFT *Capt Myron Brown is congratulated by Gen Sweetser after completing his 50th combat mission over enemy territory. Capt Brown flew a full tour with the 730th BS from bases in Japan and Pusan East (Myron Brown)*

the war was also called on to fly its fair share of daylight bombing sorties. From February 1951 onwards, this mission became extremely dangerous for B-26 crews venturing north of Pyongyang, as the area was now patrolled by MiG-15s. The slow Invader was 'easy pickings' for the Soviet jet.

Lt Calvin Bradley, from the 13th BS, remembers a bombing mission that he flew to the North Korean capital when just 48 hours away from finishing his tour;

'The C-54 was still two days away from arriving to take us out when the call went out for a maximum effort daytime bombing mission over Pyongyang. I guess the planners figured we would take them by surprise and have point-blank accuracy at an altitude of just 8500 ft. The B-29s had been chewed up the last time they tried a daytime mission over Pyongyang.

'Our 13th Squadron commander was in a bind. Many of the replacement pilots were inexperienced and untried, whilst others that had just arrived were World War 2 types that had not yet finished checking out in the B-26. Lt Col Belser called in all of the guys that had finished their tours and told us about the frag order for the next day's mission. He asked us if we would be willing

to fly one more mission, and that he would not hold it against any of us should we refuse. Well, all the "Tigers" took the bait and volunteered. Our 13th Squadron would put up 15 Invaders, plus a spare. The CO would fly lead.

'We took off first, and the other two squadrons followed with a maximum efforts also. It was strictly a 3rd BW show.

'Our aircraft, flown by Lt Jim Becker, was something of a gas hog. The weather began at six-tenths cloud coverage and got worse en route. The CO told us to tighten up the formation and not to break away or we'd never be able to rejoin in time. We stayed in close, weaving and corkscrewing between cloud layers. At times, I would lose sight of almost all of the closest aircraft. If all of our B-26s had been parked on the ground in the same formation, I could have hopped from plane to plane – and I mean every one of them!

'Those guys were as cool as ice. I was too busy doing follow navigation to maintain any position, copying headings, air speed, altitudes and fuel readings, and doing my best to keep my hands from shaking, and responding on the intercom in what I hoped was a clear and steady tone of voice.

BELOW A load of four 1000-lb GP bombs indicated that this particular B-26 was either going after a major rail centre or tunnels, as both targets required serious destructive power. On most missions against truck convoys, or when making rail cuts, the bombs typically used were 500-lb GPs. This aircraft was from the 3rd BW's 731st BS, based at Iwakuni AB. The unit became the 90th BS soon after this photograph was taken, the 'new' squadron specialising in the night interdiction mission (Andy Anderson)

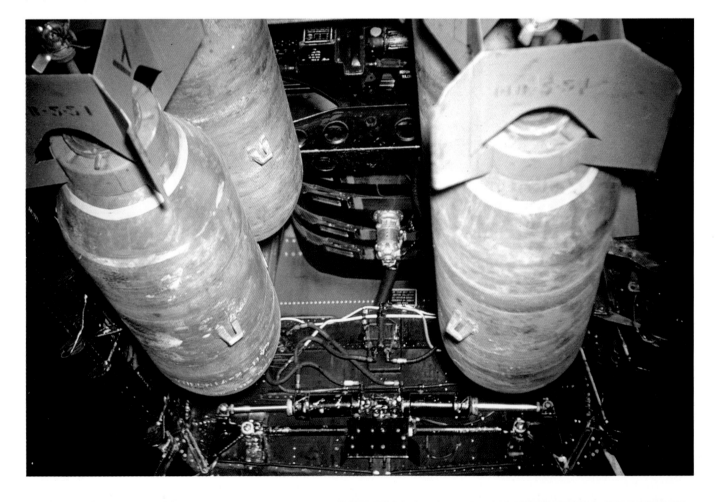

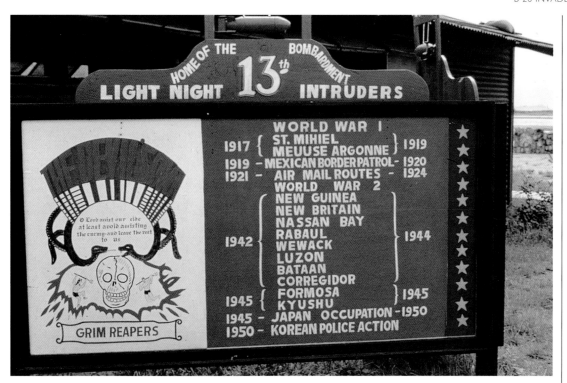

ABOVE LEFT *The 13th BS 'Grim Reapers' was one of the oldest units in the air force, and it proudly displayed its lineage on an intricately-detailed sign strategically placed in front of the squadron's operations shack. Remaining in the Pacific after World War 2 and then Korea, the 13th went on to become one of the first USAF units to see action in Vietnam in the mid-1960s, flying B-57s out of Clark AB, in the Philippines (Robert Sedgwick)*

LEFT *One of the largest bomb dumps in South Korea was located at Pusan East. Sited less than a mile away from a major sea port, the dump was kept re-supplied by the numerous munitions ships that regularly docked after crossing the Pacific from the USA. South Korean labourers usually manned the bomb trucks, and this ordnance has just been dropped off as a single load for a 17th BW B-26. With the bombs in place, the armourers would then arrive at the dispersal and load up each aircraft. The mix of bombs employed depended on the type of target each Invader was going after (Will Plentl)*

'Our last turn point prior to the IP was right on the edge of the restricted area around the site where the peace talks were being held. The weather had gotten so bad that the other two squadrons behind us had already broken formation, and they went on to hit secondary "targets of opportunity".

'I was really praying that the target would be clear, and it was. We took the flak batteries by surprise! There were over a hundred 105 mm anti-aircraft batteries around the target area, and they had their fuses set for the much higher altitudes used by the B-29s. We were just about over the target before they got our altitude zeroed in. Then it started to get sticky! It sounded like we were driving too fast on loose gravel.

'We made it in formation across the target in the daylight! Our bombs were right on the mark, and we headed for home. The strike photos later evaluated by Bomb Damage Assessment showed that 98 per cent of the bombs were on target. We had F-86 top cover and some Australian Meteors. We were very low on fuel, and had to land at Seoul before going on to Kunsan. The CO was grateful for our help, and since our records were already closed out and forwarded to our next duty station, we didn't even get credit for the mission.'

When the war began, the North Korean Peoples' Air Force had a large number of Russian-built Yak types in service that posed only a marginal threat to UN assets. Between the F-80s, F-82s and F-51s, they were soon rendered ineffective. Indeed, B-26 crews rarely encountered them during either day or night operations. However, the enemy found an effective way to use a biplane trainer aircraft against some UN air bases.

The antiquated Polikarpov Po-2 was sent south of the 38th Parallel at night to drop hand grenades on parked aircraft, and to keep air force personnel from getting a good night's sleep. These nuisance raids mirrored those flown by Japanese 'Washing Machine Charlies' throughout the Pacific during World War 2. The sorties became so frequent that the US Navy's sole ace during the Korean War claimed nothing but Po-2s while flying the F4U-5N nightfighter version of the Corsair.

A Polikarpov biplane was also destroyed by 8th BS Invader pilot Capt Richard Heyman, who takes up the story;

'On the night of 23 June 1951, we had been on a night strafing mission up north. The aircraft we were flying was a real gas guzzler, so we were returning early, and still had some of our 0.5-in ammunition left. We had package guns under the wings and the turret in back. As we were getting close to Kunsan (our base), we heard the controller, "Dentist", calling for any aircraft in the vicinity of Seoul that had any ammo left. We answered, and he immediately vectored us toward a slow-flying bogey. As we got closer, he advised us to descend to a lower altitude (about 1000 ft), and what really shocked me was his request for us to slow down to about 100 knots! There was no way we could stay airborne at that speed!

'When we were close enough, I slowed to about 130 knots, dropped the flaps and gear and opened the cowl flaps and bomb-bay doors. All of this was to give us more drag. I shoved the RPM up to a high setting, but left the manifold pressure down to maintain flying speed and control. The time was slightly past midnight, and the moon was out. All three of us were straining our eyes looking for "Charlie". We had dropped down below the radar coverage. After a short while we saw this biplane, and radioed the controller to make sure it was the intruder we were after. He confirmed it.

'The Po-2 was flying 180 degrees to our heading, so we whipped around and gave chase. He did a good job of evading us by turning into us so we would overshoot him. After about ten minutes of this "cat and mouse" game, we

thought we had lost him. Suddenly, we spotted him right down on the deck, flying over a river and going between banks. I guess the pilot didn't realise that the water reflecting in the moonlight made him clearly stand out.

'I pulled around in a steep bank and gave him a burst of 0.5-in that raked all over his fuselage. He went down in seconds. Somehow, the pilot and gunner must have gotten out, because there were no bodies found in, or near, the wreckage. We went on to land and refuel at Kimpo, before flying on to Kunsan. The news had travelled fast, and we were allowed to make several low victory passes over the base.'

As mentioned earlier in this volume, the 12th TRS probably kept the lowest profile of any squadron serving in Korea. Flying RB-26Cs, its record over enemy territory at night was second to none. However, the unit's mission differed from the bomber squadrons in that the 12th was tasked with providing much needed intelligence for the FEAF on what the enemy was up to after the day fighter-bombers had been 'put away for the night'.

One of the experienced Bombardier/Navigators that flew with the 12th TRS was 1Lt W J Moulton, who gives some insight into the aircraft that he flew, and what the unit did during those long nights over enemy territory;

BELOW *Many of the flightcrews from the 8th and 13th BSs were trained to perform minor maintenance on the top 0.5-in machine gun turret. Both the dorsal and ventral barbettes proved very effective in combat, especially when the Invader pulled up following a firing pass and the gunner rotated his turrets to face rearward, thus allowing him to strafe as the B-26 flew away! (LeRoy Bain)*

'Our RB-26s were mostly modified C-models, with the glass nose and minus the 0.5-in machine guns. Powered by two 2800 hp Pratt & Whitney engines, the aircraft's maximum speed was supposed to be 373 mph. However, the further modification of removing the rear turrets and guns boosted that speed up to about 425 mph.

'Our regular aircraft had a Norden bombsight in the nose, but it was very seldom used by the navigator. He was really the "eyes" of the mission, and tried to remain visual on all missions to bring back "sightings" to the intelligence people.

'We had a compartment with added bombing and navigational equipment installed where the rear turret had been. We had a SHOrt range RAdar Navigation (SHORAN) set and a LOng RAnge Navigational (LORAN) set. Also, bomb-rack controls were fitted for better manipulation of individual bomb drops, rather than the rack controls in the front of the aircraft.

'Basically, we had a three-fold mission. The first was to fly routes along both coasts and up the centre of the peninsula. The east coast route would sometimes take us so far north that we were able to see the rotating beacon at the airport at Vladivostok, in Russia! The west coast route would take us up to the mouth of the Yalu River. The centre route covered the main roads into Pyongyang from the north and south.

'These routes were covered nightly for troop and equipment movements. Any sightings were immediately called in to the interdiction B-26s. These sightings would then be part of our second mission, for we would remain over the target until the Invaders from the 3rd or 17th BWs arrived. When they were ready, we would go in with flares and light the area up. After they had completed bombing and strafing, we would then go back in to get pictures of the target for Bomb Damage Assessment (BDA).

'The third regular mission saw us taking pictures of known airfields that were bombed during the day, but due to "Coolie" labour forces, could be repaired fast enough to be used at night. Once in a while we would photograph targets that other services might want pictures of for their plans. The average duration of our missions was about two hours.'

BELOW *The illustrious history of the 3rd BW was well known to both its members and the press. Nevertheless, there were signs posted all over its Kunsan base that reminded those who may have forgotten! This particular one tracks the wing's history from World War I all the way through to the Korean War (Chester LeRoy)*

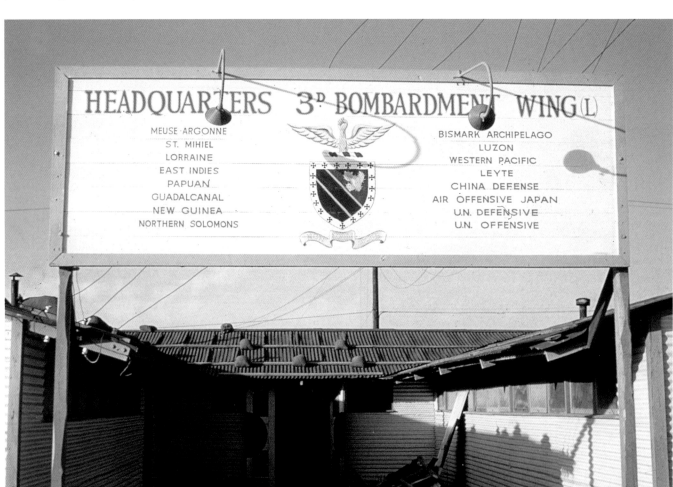

LEFT *In an effort to deter UN aircraft from strafing, the North Koreans stretched thick steel cables between a number of the narrow valleys 'up north'. Despite communist hopes that unsuspecting fighter-bombers would hit the cable and crash, this particular B-26 flew through a wire and just kept right on going! However, on other occasions F-51 Mustangs and at least one F-82 were brought down by the cables, with the respective pilots being killed (H A Gamblin)*

RIGHT *The maintenance crews did what they had to in order to 'keep 'em flying'. Here, the B-26 in the background is undergoing repairs to its right main landing gear (note the jack), whilst the aircraft in the foreground is in the process of having a battle-damaged horizontal stabiliser replaced. All of these repairs would be considered routine, and were usually accomplished out on the ramp between missions. Both of these Invaders are from the 13th BS (Joe Lobosco)*

BELOW *The pilot positions his B-26 immediately below the slipstream of his flight leader as a formation of 8th BS bombers heads north. Typically, on daylight formation bomb drops the aircraft would be spread out more than is shown here. Once the war ended, much formation flying of this nature took place during the hours of daylight, giving crews ample opportunity to take photos of their aircraft 'on the wing' (David Botto)*

ABOVE *Aircraft in the 'bone yards' at most of the bases in South Korea were picked clean, especially where older, outdated piston-engined types were being operated. Indeed, spare parts for Corsairs, Mustangs and Invaders were all but non-existent by the final months of the war. These two B-26s formerly flew with the 3rd BW, prior to becoming primary sources for the spare parts needed to keep frontline aircraft operational. They had probably crash-landed at Kunsan due to battle damage, or had been shot up so badly that they were deemed to be beyond repair (Hans Petermann)*

LEFT *Sgt Robert McDonald (729th BS) replaces an exhaust stack on the port engine of his B-26. Occasionally, the sheer volume of minor repairs required was so great that it was impossible to render the aircraft serviceable in time for the next night mission. However, the groundcrews usually achieved minor mechanical 'miracles' in the crudest conditions imaginable, and most B-26s were back in the air within 48 hours (Robert Hansen)*

This panoramic view of the Pusan East flightline reveals just how inhospitable the terrain was at the northern end of the runway. Mountains ringed the base on three sides, with the harbour being the only safe way out (to the south) for a heavily-laden B-26. If a pilot lost an engine on take-off when fully loaded, he had little option but to ditch the bomber – making sure not to hit the ammunition ships that were anchored off the end of the runway! These red-trimmed Invaders are from the 37th BS (David Whiting)

RIGHT The 8th BS proudly showed off its past history on this sign, posted in front of the squadron operations block at Kunsan AB. The 8th would convert over to the new B-57 Canberra bomber not long after returning from the Korean War. Remaining within the 3rd BW, the unit would fly the Martin-built bomber from Clark AB, in the Philippines (Jake Clements)

BELOW RIGHT As one B-26 pilots stated, 'You haven't lived until you fly a daylight, low-level attack using several aircraft at the same time'. This scene depicts just that, Lt Dennis Boyle having captured the drama of multiple bomb blasts going off as his Invader heads into the target area. Beneath the smoke is a large ammunition dump and truck depot, which erupted with numerous secondary explosions. Shock waves from the exploding ordnance made bomb aiming for the trailing aircraft an almost impossible task (Dennis Boyle)

OPPOSITE A trio of 728th BS pilots pose for the camera in front of their operations shack at Miho, in Japan. The squadron emblem was the 'Flying Cannibal', and the unit was controlled by the 452nd BW. The ubiquitous A-2 leather flying jacket was seldom, if ever, worn operationally by B-26 aircrewmen in Korea because of the bitterly cold weather. Dedicated winter gear was the clothing of choice, as shown here by the two pilots suited up and ready to fly (Dennis Boyle)

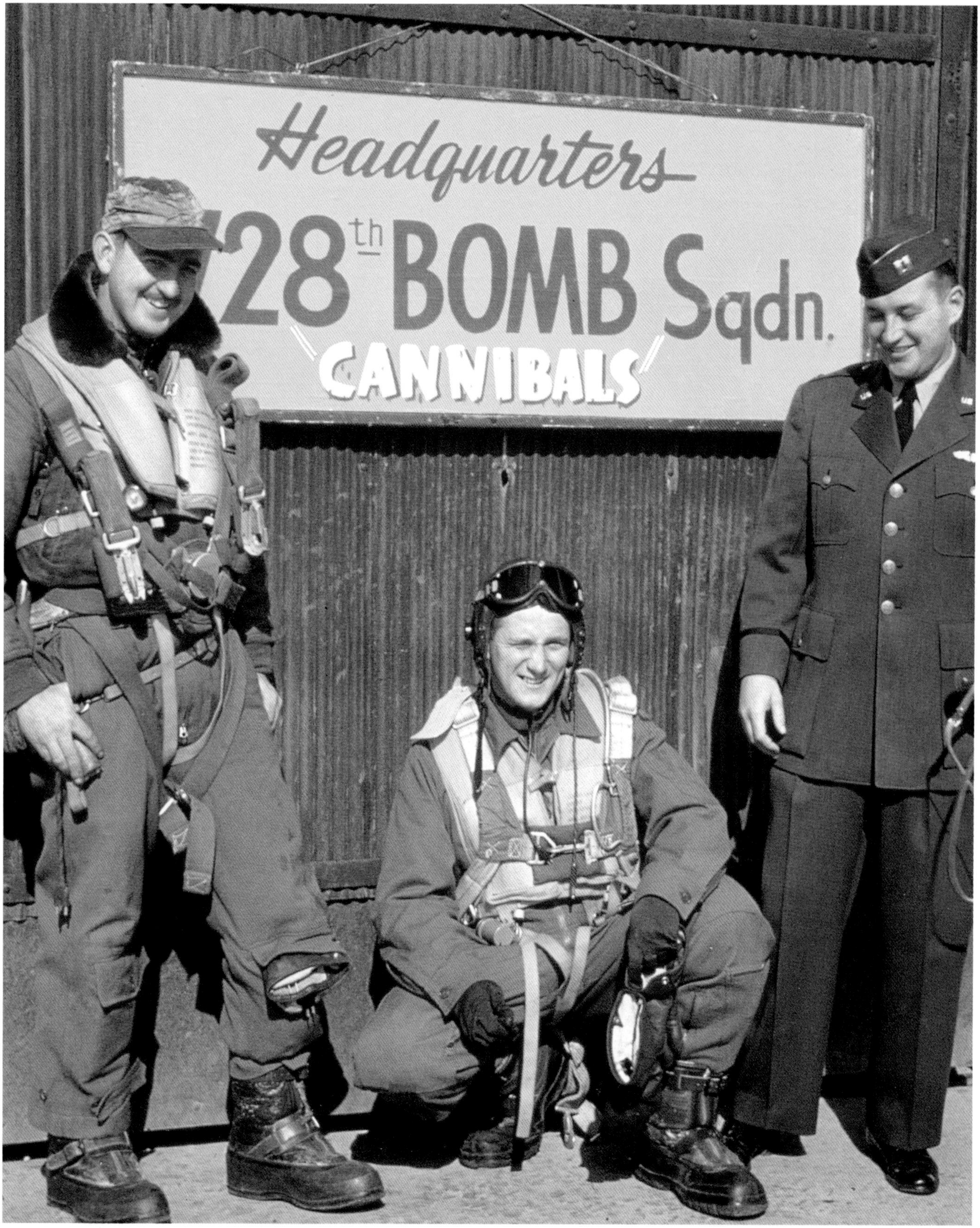
Headquarters
28th BOMB Sqdn.
CANNIBALS

MAIN PICTURE *It is late afternoon on the 8th BS's flightline, and groundcrews are going over some minor details with the aircraft that are scheduled to fly the impending night sorties. The 8th flew the first bombing mission of the war, and it would also fly the last. The B-26s parked off in the background (with white trim) are from the 90th BS (Cale Herry)*

INSET LEFT *This veteran B-26B was nicknamed BIG CHIEF, and it had been with the 13th BS since the early days of the war. Hit by flak on the mission flown immediately prior to this photo being taken, the bomber had suffered a holed right oil reservoir. This in turn meant that the pilot had to feather the bomber's right propeller and shut down the associated engine prior to arriving back at Kunsan. With no ordnance on board, the B-26 was easily controlled with one good engine (John Harris)*

INSET RIGHT *For a brief period there were two B-26s in each of the units controlled by the 3rd BW that performed the specialised searchlight role. The mission equipment fitted under the wing in a napalm-sized tank, operating on 72 Volts of DC power and producing beams of light rated at 70,000,000 candlepower. They searchlight would be turned on for one minute and off for five so as to allow the unit to cool down. The beam had a range of two miles, and was used to illuminate truck convoys. One strafing pass could be made while the light was on, and the system proved less than successful primarily because flak gunners could easily locate attacking B-26s (J Harris)*

CHAPTER THREE

COUNTERING INCREASED SUPPLY EFFORTS

Once the massive Chinese 'human wave' offensive ran out of steam in the early spring of 1951, the war's complexion changed drastically. There is no doubt that the high command within the Chinese military figured that the UN forces could be ejected from the Korean Peninsula through manpower alone. And despite having seen at first-hand the effect that air power had on the North Korean military, the Chinese army still entered the war believing in their invincibility – and with no real air power.

UN fighter-bombers wrecked any chances the Chinese had of moving en masse during the day. Troops, therefore, had to move during the night and camouflage themselves during the day, with the latter proving to be an almost impossible task due to the large numbers involved.

By April 1951 it was apparent that the Chinese could not support the manpower needed to push UN forces any further south. This left communist army commanders with two choices. Firstly, they could hold what ground they had and negotiate a ceasefire, with the border drawn near the original 38th Parallel. Or secondly, they could try and move enough supplies and ammunition during the night to sustain a series of offensives designed to drive UN forces south a few miles at a time. They chose the latter option. This put tremendous pressure on the B-26 units, for they were given the job of shutting down the re-supply network!

Chinese logistics experts realised that moving supplies via train involved much risk, whilst road-bed repairs took time and much manpower. The best way to win this phase of the battle was to put so many trucks on the roads that it would be impossible to keep the necessary supplies from reaching their destination. This tactic worked, but it proved costly. The communists also realised that if the trains continued to roll south, they would

RIGHT *The attrition rate among B-26s was extremely high due to their constant exposure to the best flak gunners in the Chinese army. The Douglas bombers were also constantly at the mercy of the elements, flying low-level missions in total darkness over mountainous terrain. In an effort to offset these losses, the USAF kept the bomb wings supplied with a steady flow of replacement aircraft brought in from California. Capt Al Keeler snapped this photo at Hickam AB on Hawaii in early 1953 during a transpac stop-over. These B-26s were en route to Korea, with the B-29 in the background acting as their 'mother ship'. The Boeing bomber provided accurate navigational cues to the Invader crews during the long water crossing (Al Keeler)*

LEFT *The flightcrews rode out to their aircraft via any form of motorised transport that they could find. The alternative was a tiring trek laden down with flightgear and assorted maps. At this stage in the war the 8th BS was undertaking a considerable number of daylight formation bomb drops. According to one squadron pilots, 'about ten days out of fifty were spent on this type of mission, the rest of our sorties being flown at low altitude during the night' (Bob Swanson)*

RIGHT *8th BS pilot Lt Bob Swanson holds up a new recruiting poster that the US Air Force started to use in 1953, which showed Marilyn Monroe climbing out of the cockpit of an F-86 Sabre. Needless to say, the poster generated considerable interest at the bases in Korea. This photograph was taken in March 1953 at Kunsan AB, home of the 3rd BW (Bob Swanson)*

OPPOSITE *Navigator Lt Harry Galpin poses on the flightline at Taegu in full flightgear prior to flying a daylight mission. The yellow-trimmed B-26 is from the 8th BS whilst the bomber marked in red belongs to the 13th BS (Harry Galpin)*

relieve some of the pressure from the truck convoys – Invader crews still considered a locomotive kill as the ultimate prize in the nocturnal arena.

Lt Bernard B Waller of the 8th BS was a navigator/bombardier during this crucial pahse of the war, and here he remembers his 30th mission over North Korea. As usual, his crew was going after trains or rail cuts up in the 'Purple' sectors;

'We were briefed and assigned to make railroad cuts up in the "Purple-11" area of North Korea. There wasn't much moonlight at 1 am that night, but when we arrived in the target area, there was a single locomotive making a break for a nearby tunnel. My pilot dove on it and sent two-500-lb bombs into the locomotive at the entrance to the tunnel. The pull-up felt like 6gs, with the mountain coming right at us. This had to hurt their supply efforts for a short while.

'Our attack awakened their anti-aircraft gunners, because big red balls and white streaks started following us everywhere. We, in turn, went after them with a couple of strafing runs and one bomb. This quietened them down, and we got down to our real business of rail cutting.

'First, we dropped about five flares at 5000 ft, and then the pilot pushed our aircraft (nicknamed *Midnite Rendezvous*) over and we dived under the flares and buried two 500-lb fuse-delay bombs into the rail bed

before the flares burned out. This proved to be a bit tricky, and it took four passes to finish off our supply of bombs and flares. Before heading back home, we covered the bombed-out area of track with 20-lb anti-personnel bombs that would explode on physical contact.

'On our final pass we dropped leaflets that warned the repair crews of the danger they would face when fixing the track. This technique severely handicapped the ability of the enemy to move supplies by rail.'

Originally, the Invader had been sent to Korea as a low/medium altitude light bomber that was to be used exclusively for daylight missions. At the start of the war no one could have predicted that the B-26 would be employed principally as a night intruder, and that day missions would prove to be few and far between.

In light of this radical operational change, both the 3rd and 452nd BWs attempted to formulate a manual on night tactics, but there was no way of assessing just how effective these missions were at stopping truck convoys. No aerial photography was being made available to the wings that would substantiate claims from the night before. The single RB-26C unit in-theate had the capability to take such photos at night, but had found it difficult to zero in on the exact position where the attack had taken place.

When Fifth Air Force HQ saw what the Chinese were attempting to do, they initiated a major campaign

The wear and tear inflicted on the B-26s in Korea was exceptionally high, as some aircraft flew every night. Standard service intervals were strictly observed in-theatre, and should an aircraft have survived long enough to require depot-level maintenance, it would be flown back to Japan. Here, its engines would be detached, and either comprehensively reworked or replaced altogether. Airframe checks were also carried out, and any temporary 'quick-fix' flak damage repairs were made good. Finally, the aircraft was repainted, although the nose-art was always left untouched. Flightcrews, meanwhile, would take advantage of these trips by getting in a little R&R in Japan. Having enjoyed a lay over of a few days, the crew would typically return to their Korean base in a recently reworked Invader. The crew of this battle-scared 13th BS B-26C are seen preparing for a long overwater flight from their base at Kunsan (K-8) to the maintenance facility at Johnson AB, on the east coast of Japan (Al Keeler)

ABOVE *This unique sign was erected by the radar technicians at Kunsan, the photograph being taken right after the 3rd BW had settled in to what could only be described as shabby facilities. Within six months, a large number of permanent buildings had been erected, protecting most of the support personnel from the elements during the harsh winters. The wing shared Kunsan with Marine nightfighter squadron VMF(N)-513 (Frank Longden)*

against the movement of supplies by the enemy, code-named Operation *Strangle*. This commenced in May/June 1951, with the primary targets being the road traffic on seven main supply routes that converged on the frontline area from the north. Part of this plan called the B-26s and Marine F4U-5Ns to patrol specific areas at night.

Flying out of Kunsan, the 3rd BW was made responsible for covering the main supply routes in western North Korea, whilst the 452nd's B-26s would patrol the supply routes to the east. This left VMF(N)-513's Corsairs to intercept anything that was moving close to and slightly north of the frontline. If supplies did get through, the F4Us would work with flare-ships to foil any attempts to unload the freight.

It was during this period that the various routes were identified by colours. 'Purple' routes, for example ran deep into North Korea, and included the mountainous region that was known as 'MiG Alley'.

For safety reasons, as well as to maintain effectiveness, the B-26s continued to work as 'singles', operating to a tight schedule that kept an Invader up over certain areas

for the entire night. This resulted in a lot of the convoys moving slowly, or left them practically at a standstill. During the cold winter months, the intervals between Invaders was timed at 30 minutes, whilst in the summer, this figure came down to every 15 minutes.

Strangle also saw the debut of an innovative device in the form of a powerful searchlight fitted under the wing of the B-26. Its tenure was short-lived, however, for crews found that communist flak gunners relied on the lights to pin-point otherwise 'invisible' B-26s in the night sky.

These searchlights had belonged to the US Navy, who had fitted them to airships in an effort to flush out enemy submarines during World War 2. When they arrived in Korea, 3rd BW commander, Col Nils Ohman, ruled that there would only be two aircraft per squadron equipped with the lights.

The searchlight themselves were packaged into a bolt-on external store about the size of a napalm bomb, which produced considerable drag, and duly cut down the B-26's range and loiter time over the target area. Due to the extremely high amount of heat generated by the

light, it could only be used for about 50 seconds before it had to be turned off for five minutes to allow it to cool down.

Despite the searchlights only being used for a short time, there is one episode involving the 'weapon' that has to be told. It concerns the exploits of Capt John S Walmsley of the 8th BS, who received the Medal of Honor whilst flying an Invader equipped with 'night lights'.

During a routine night mission, Walmsley and his crew stopped a convoy north of Hwangju with 500-lb fire bombs. They made about ten passes over the column of stalled trucks, employing the searchlight intermittently. Throughout the mission, an officer sat in the nose of the B-26C reporting that the searchlight was literally scaring the truck drivers to death, for they had driven off into ditches or had collisions with each other. It had been a great success, but two nights later it would prove fatal.

On his very next mission, on 14 September 1951, Capt Walmsley spotted and illuminated a train near Yangdok. Having spent all of his ammunition and ordnance, he called in another B-26 that was in the vicinity. His plan was to illuminate the train for the second aircraft. This time, the enemy gunners were ready, and they focused their fire on the searchlight. Walmsley's aircraft was shot down and the crew perished. For this heroic act, Capt Walmsley was posthumously awarded the Medal of Honor.

Both tactical and technical complications effectively killed off the searchlight, and after a month's use, it was withdrawn from the frontline B-26 force.

Lt John W Harris of the 13th BS flew Invaders during the searchlight's brief tenure, but never had to fly any missions with the device. He later commented;

'The use of powerful searchlights at low-level didn't seem to me to be a very good idea, and it was a controversial one to say the least. They were a lot of trouble, and had only a very short "on" time because of the terrific heat they generated.

'I felt that the enemy gunners could find us easily enough without giving them any help! A fellow pilot in the squadron, Lt Stanley J Murphy, flew several missions with one. He said you could say goodbye to whatever visibility

ABOVE *Dressed for the coldest weather imaginable, these aircrewmen from the 13th BS prepare to 'mount up' in preparation for an early evening mission. On the far right is navigator Lt Sigmund Alexander, who flew a long tour out of Kunsan with the squadron. This photo was taken in February 1953 (Sigmund Alexander)*

you had when the light came on. Reflection from the haze must have been pretty bad. I felt fortunate in that I never had to fly one of these missions. The light probably worked well during cold weather when there was less haze. The air got pretty thick sometimes in the summer.'

With a significant number of the north/south roads being grouped in close proximity to each other, it was easy for the B-26s to work both at the same time, as Lt Hans Petermann, a bombardier/navigator with the 8th BS, recalls. This particular mission saw his crew patrolling the roads between Sariwon and Pyongyang, which was always busy due to it being one of the enemy's main supply routes;

'We were flying in a hard nose B-model and it was clear and bright with a full moon and lots of snow on the ground, so visibility was excellent. We couldn't find any traffic on our route, but heard an aircraft from another squadron reporting that he had attacked a train on their route north of Chinnampo. After they called in and cleared the area, our pilot, Lt John Schmitt, radioed and received permission to go into that area for a "look-see".

'We easily spotted the train, as it was standing still. It was a locomotive, with several empty gondola cars with snow in them and a caboose. It showed no signs of having been damaged. John immediately made several low passes at the train but without success. We finally left after expending all of our ordnance, with the train still on the tracks. We reported to our outbound controller the map co-ordinates of the train, and the negative results.

'There was a long pause and then a request for confirmation of the co-ordinates. This was given, and then another pause ensued. Back came "that train was reported destroyed with fires and explosions by so-and-so squadron". Schmitt replied that the train was still on the tracks with snow in the gondola cars, so there was no way that there could have been any fires. We received the same dubious response during our debriefing. The next day we were chewed out for dropping our bombs too low as evidenced by bomb fragments in the bottom of our aircraft. The type of bombs we carried were not supposed to be released below 500 ft.'

This type of mission was commonplace in that the results were not worthy of the effort put in by the air- and groundcrews. The number of missions flown where there just weren't any targets to be hit were probably too numerous to count.

On a number of missions B-26s just disappeared following the loss of radio contact. These bombers had more than likely been hit by anti-aircraft fire and crashed before the crew had had time to radio any information on their fate. Lt Petermann recalls one such mission that could have ended in instant disaster for him and his crew;

'One night I was flying in the back of a B-26C as radar operator. On climb-out after take-off, I smelled gas fumes and reported it to the pilot. A few minutes later it got worse, and I reported to the pilot that I was going onto 100 per cent oxygen. He immediately became concerned and asked for further information. At that point my interphone transmission went out and I could not respond. Nothing I tried restored communication with him over the 'phones. I could hear him and the rest of the crew and he became worried that I had passed out from the fumes.

'He initiated a return to base and told everyone not to activate any switches. I finally thought of trying to communicate by flashlight. I could see the props from my windows and I flashed my light on them. After several tries, the pilot saw the flashes. We then communicated by my flashing on the left prop for a "yes" to his question and on the right prop for a "no". He was satisfied that I was okay, but that the excessive fumes situation still existed.

'We landed back at Kunsan, pulled off the runway and shut down. Emergency personnel arrived, and when the bomb-bay doors were opened, gasoline poured out onto the ramp. I would say we were very lucky nothing worse happened. We debriefed and thought that our night was finished, and that we could avail ourselves of a post-mission "relaxer". No such luck! We were assigned the back-up aircraft and went ahead with a full mission. If a spark or something had ignited the gas in our original aircraft, we would have exploded in a giant fireball, with no chance of letting anyone know what had happened!'

The final six months of 1951 had taken a heavy toll on the B-26 inventory. However, the Chinese offensive had been curtailed, but this in turn meant that the enemy was bringing in more guns to protect its established supply lines. By the spring of 1952, the number of operational B-26s in Korea was at an all-time low. This was due not only to operational losses but also a lack of spare parts. The total inventory in the Far East had dropped to 187 Invaders, and many of these were simply worn out.

Realising the seriousness of this situation, the FEAF reacted swiftly, and by September 1952 both the 3rd and 17th BWs had been returned to their full complement of 48 aircraft per wing (16 per squadron).

A paucity of aircraft was not the only problem facing the B-26 community. As the war ground on, the inexperienced crewmembers that were rotating into the frontline force lacked sufficient training to perform the low-level night intruder work. The direct result of this was a higher than normal loss rate in operationbal accidents. In light of this, Fifth Air Force made the decision to group all experienced night intruder aircrews into just one squadron per wing. The 13th BS was selected for the 3rd BW and the 37th BS for the 17th BW.

BELOW *This 37th BS B-26C is seen at K-9 in April 1953, having been loaded with a variety of ordnance including fire bombs, flares and 500-lb GP bombs. Maintenance crews are wrapping up their work on the right engine before the crew arrives in the late afternoon to fly the first mission of the night. At this late stage in the war, a 'maximum effort' was undertaken by both B-26 wings each and every night in order to prevent the Chinese from making a final push southward in the lead up to the ceasefire (Dexter Martin)*

Although the vast majority of B-26 sorties saw aircraft going after enemy transportation, other types of missions were occasionally performed, with spectacular results. One such assignment concerned the co-ordination of a precision attack on searchlights and anti-aircraft batteries surrounding the massive powerplant at Sinuiju, on the Yalu River. The aim of this mission was to allow a B-29 bomber stream to hit the target unmolested. The Invader crews did exactly what they were asked to do, and no B-29s were lost on either of the two missions flown against this high-value target.

Lt Glenn A Phipps, who flew with the 13th BS, recounts the details of just such a mission against one of the largest power-generating plants in the Far East;

'It seems that Bomber Command had been given the job of levelling this plant. Our aerial photo reconnaissance showed that most of the searchlights and guns were up in the hills on the south side of the river. As we were strictly forbidden to fly over China, this meant that the B-29s had to make their bomb run right down the corridor of enemy guns.

'Bomber Command was planning a bomber stream with five minute intervals between aircraft. This would allow all of the enemy lights and guns to concentrate on one bomber at a time, so the B-29 guys wanted a major diversion, and that is where the B-26s came in. We were asked to provide six Invaders to fly suppression while the bombers were overhead. We agreed!

'Six hard-nose B-models were selected for their 14 forward-firing guns. We also had them loaded up with anti-personnel fragmentation bombs, which came in sticks of six. Using piano wire, we double-hung two sticks to each of the bomb bay shackles. It was believed that the combination of these two weapons would do the job. We then selected six of our most experienced crews. Our plan was to arrive just prior to the first B-29, and start our suppression mission as the enemy turned on their search-lights. Since the lights and guns were set up as integral units, going after the lights as they came on would also suppress the guns! The bomber stream was planned to cover a one-and-a-half-hour period.

'Our six Invaders were scheduled to spend 20 minutes in the target area apiece. We executed our plan perfectly, and none of the bombers was shot down. We dropped all of our ordnance, and although we had no way of knowing how effective we were against the guns, we sure knew when we took out a searchlight!

'We received a "well-done" signal from Bomber Command, and another mission was immediately sched-uled. However, when we arrived in the target area, we got a big surprise! The guns and lights had all been shifted over to the north side of the river, which was off limits. The first bomber was already approaching the target. We had to make a decision, and it was left up to the individual pilots, for if we had discussed it on the radios the mission would have automatically been scrubbed. We all did the

BELOW Only a handful of these modified B-26s were used in Korea. Part of the 'Red Bird' project, they were fitted with experimental heat-seeking equipment in the nose to enable crews to detect vehicles and trains on the ground at night. The device proved particularly successful in the search for locomotives, which gave off large amounts of heat. A truly top secret project, the aircraft so modified usually had their noses kept covered up with a sheet of canvas when parked on the ramp during the day. This example, minus sheeting, was photographed at Kunsan in January 1953 wearing the colours of the 13th BS (Sigmund Alexander)

same thing, and the lights and guns were taken out. The B-29s got in and finished the job with no losses.

'At the debriefing, all targets were reported as being on the south side as before, and the B-29 guys never said a word to the contrary. We received another "well done" from Bomber Command. The Chinese did not complain about the attack either, and we were left unaware of just how effective the B-29s had been. It was simply a case of doing what was necessary to protect the bomber crews.'

Fewer and fewer daylight missions were flown by the B-26s as the war wound down. When such sorties were tasked, crews usually flew in large formations in an effort to respond to a newly-discovered troop concentration or supply dump. Invaders could put more ordnance on a target than any other type of aircraft based near to the frontline. To call in a B-29 strike would have involved a lengthy lead time, as they had to be loaded and then flown all the way from either Okinawa or Japan.

Navigator Lt Andy Bender recalls a high altitude mission he was involved in with the 3rd BW;

'Some missions were flown at high altitude (for the B-26) at about 10,000 ft in support of either frontline troops or against important targets. The frontline support sorties were called "Q" drops. We would be vectored by

ground radar to a spot where the bomb trajectory had been determined, and we would then release the ordnance by voice command. When operating against enemy troops, the ordnance of choice was usually the 250-lb frag bomb.

'When we were sent up against buildings, we used SHORAN. This system saw two ground radio station signals being displayed as blips on a three-inch screen fitted into the aircraft. When we got within ten miles of the blips intersecting, we would open the bomb-bay doors, and when the blips met, the bombs would release. We never got to see the results from either type of drop, but sometimes we would get damage assessment from the ground. On one occasion, a few of our crews got lucky and caught Chinese troops massing for an attack. The resulting body count exceeded 3000.'

On 27 July 1953 the first major conflict within the confines of the Cold War came to an end. Like all of the wars that would follow, it finished in stalemate. However, the war in Korea had had a significant impact on the United States military.

Though off to a slow start, jet warfare had matured into a force to be reckoned with, rapidly changing the make up of the USAF in particular. Speed was life, and as

ABOVE *Of all the areas worked by the B-26s at night, the most dangerous were known as 'Purple Sectors'. This code basically translated into sectors in and around 'MiG Alley'. It was in this area that most of the convoys and critical supply loads originated, and it was heavily defended with searchlights and flak sites. About the only consolation was that the B-26s were working at too low an altitude to be intercepted by the nightflying MiG-15s that patrolled the area! Preparing for a mission into the 'Purple Sector', this 13th BS aircraft is loaded with several types of ordnance (Corky Sumner)*

Two B-26s from the 90th BS return from a pre-dawn mission, heading south along the west coast of Korea. They are approaching Kunsan AB, which was located right on the coastal plain bordered by the East China Sea. This photograph was taken in the final weeks of the war (Doug Garno)

RIGHT *Still wearing their 'Mae Wests', the pilot and his gunner solve a last minute technical problem with the top turret prior to the mission being flown. Another B-26 tasked with flying one of the first sorties of the night taxies out for take-off behind the stationary Invader. Note the paved taxyway laid at Kunsan during the latter stages of the war. At this time the base was still also home to a Marine night-fighter unit and an F-84 group (James Council)*

BELOW *Being the CO's aircraft, there was never any doubt as to who would usually be assigned to fly the CHADWICK series of B-26s. THE 7TH CHADWICK was the mount of 13th BS CO, Lt Col Robert Fortney. And despite sharing the same nickname, none of the previous CHADWICKs boasted such an elaborate paint job (Robert Fortney)*

soon as one type of jet fighter became operational, its replacement was already well under development. The advent of the air-to-air missile had made old style dogfighting virtually a thing of the past, whilst the service introduction of surface-to-air missiles put all aircraft at risk, forcing a drastic change in mission doctrine.

However, all this lay in the immediate future, and on the final night of war in Korea, it was the Douglas B-26 Invader that ruled the skies 'up north'. The aircraft had consistently 'clogged up' the logistics support that the Chinese army needed so badly, and the crews were still prosecuting targets as the final hours of war ticked away.

Late in the afternoon of that last day, Thunderjets attacked all the serviceable airfields in North Korea. They stayed on station until sunset in an effort to prevent communist forces from bringing in significant numbers of aircraft just prior to the ceasefire. As soon as darkness set in, the 3rd and 17th BWs took over, going about their business as if it was just another night 'on the job'.

UN intelligence indicated that the communists could still launch a last minute all-out aerial attack on the key jet bases in South Korea, so all four F-86 Sabre wings in-theatre moved half of their aircraft to alternate bases further south as a precaution. Meanwhile, the F-94Bs of the 319th All Weather Squadron and the F3D Skyknights of VMF(N)-513 set up counter-air patrols which would put them in a position to intercept a large incoming force should it be detected.

A major bomb strike was also organised for the B-29s of the 19th BG, which would make a SHORAN attack on Sinuiju Airfield. This mission was scrubbed, however, as the ceasefire came into effect before the bombers could reach their target.

As the final minutes ticked off, two aircraft remained north of the bombline, and both were B-26s. The pilot of the 8th BS aircraft that dropped the last bombs of the war was Lt Donald W Mansfield, who recalls;

'It had been decided by HQ Fifth Air Force that since the 8th Squadron dropped the first bombs of the war (37 months prior), it would be fitting for the 8th to drop the final bomb. Col E B LeBailly, 3rd BW CO, selected our crew to do the honours.

BELOW Following a couple of nights off the 37th BS mission roster, 2Lts Dan Paveo (left) and Don Nation are ready to get back into action. This photograph was taken in the early summer of 1953, and both men were still flying with the squadron when the war ended (Dan Paveo)

'Our target was to be a suspected build-up of supplies just north of the bombline. Such build-ups had been going on all day, since all movement of troops, equipment and supplies was to cease at 2200 hours. We took off from Kunsan AB at 2015 hours. We checked in with our controller, who was experiencing radar problems. We were to drop our bombs from an altitude of 8000 ft. By the time the controller got everything squared away, we were still 12 miles south of the bombline and the time was 2125 hours.

'Fifth Air Force had stated that they did not want any aircraft crossing north of the line after 2130 hours. We had to radio in and get permission to proceed with the mission, and we got it. We locked on to the target, and at precisely 2133 hours we released our bombs. As we scanned the ground below, we could see the flashes from some sporadic shelling, but very little ground-to-air fire.

'We were impressed by how little chatter there was on the radio, and several controllers called us to wish us well. I heard the RB-26C from the 12th TRS check in as he crossed the bombline behind us. We were the last aircraft to drop a bomb, and the RB-26 was the last UN aircraft to fly north of the 38th Parallel. We dropped off a passenger at Kimpo AB and then proceeded back to Kunsan. We were, literally, the only aircraft in the air over South Korea.

'When we arrived back at Kunsan, over 200 men were waiting to meet us in the de-arming area at the end of the runway. Champagne was produced, and we all toasted each other and the truce that ended the war!

'In looking back, the war had been fought by an odd mix of jet fighters and World War 2 prop types. On the flightlines, there was a distinct contrast in what the pilots and aircrews wore. The jet "jocks" wore the hard helmets, and g-suits, whilst we B-26 pilots flew in cloth helmets with goggles and throat mikes. Much of our equipment came from the surplus stores back in the states!

'Everyone had respect for our veteran B-26s, and it was not to be a sad goodbye, because the Invader would make a valiant contribution with the Air Commandos over the jungles of Vietnam just over a decade later.'

FINAL BOMBING MISSION OF THE KOREAN WAR

Flown by the 8th BS/3rd BW
Aircraft – B-26C, nicknamed *BYE BYE BLUEBIRD*
Call Sign – 'Typhoon 73'

Aircrew

Pilot – 1Lt Donald W Mansfield
Navigator – 1Lt Billy L Ralston
Gunner – A2c Dennis J Judd
Passenger/Press Observer – Ed Hoffheim (Chief
          Korean Branch/International News Service)

OPPOSITE TOP *Three newly-overhauled 17th BW B-26s join up for the return flight to Korea from Japan. The blue trim indicates a 95th BS machine and red the 37th. In February/ March 1953 the 17th set its all-time bombing record against various targets. During this period the wing claimed more than half of the enemy vehicles destroyed by the Fifth Air Force. At the end of a two-week period (to 8 March), it was credited with 589 trucks destroyed. These figures included the tallies of all three squadrons within the wing (Henry Sanders)*

OPPOSITE BOTTOM *These support vehicles were kept very busy from late in the afternoon through until the early evening, shuttling aircrewmen out to their aircraft from the briefing and life support buildings. This pattern would be repeated, but in reverse, upon the crews' return the following morning. The vehicles shown here were exclusively assigned to the 34th BS – each of the three squadrons had their own motor pool to support operations (Will Plentl)*

LEFT *This photograph (which affords an excellent view of the Norden bombsight) was taken from the 'green house' in the nose of a 13th BS B-26C on 'finals' to Kunsan in the spring of 1953. In the event of a crash-landing, this was the least desirable place to be in an Invader (Frank Morito)*

INSET LEFT *There were numerous individual sectors that had to be worked each nightm and this meant that each squadron could have several aircraft airborne during the 'late shift'. On many occasions, a number of these B-26s would be heading home at about the same time, thus allowing them to join up after dawn and fly the last few minutes in formation, before entering the landing pattern. These 95th BS Invaders are pictured here doing just that over the Korean Straits, en route to Pusan East (Henry Sanders)*

MAIN PICTURE *A peaceful line-up of war-weary tails at Kunsan just days after the war had ended. The entire complement of 13th BS Invaders are taking the down time in their stride, for a hectic training regime would soon begin. The unit would remain on station at Kunsan until 5 October 1954, at which point the the squadron moved to Yokota AB, Japan (Albert Van Aman)*

INSET RIGHT *This 8th BS B-26 is seen carrying a practice bomb under its wing over South Korea in the late summer of 1953. The expertise of the Invader aircrews during the war can never be overstated, for they developed the ability to knock out precision targets at night from low-level. Indeed, flying at tree-top height through mountain valleys did not seem to phase them in the slightest. By the time the 3rd BW had completed its 10,000th night sortie, it had destroyed 6000 railroad cars. And in addition to this record, the wing claimed a large number of tanks, buildings and trucks, not to mention enemy personnel (John Sidirourgos)*

Early morning 'join-ups' were commonplace as the Invaders came out of their assigned patrol areas and headed for home. However, this photograph was almost certainly taken after a squadron-strength daylight bombing mission, with all of the aircraft dropping their ordnance on the leader's signal. Around 28 B-26s can be seen in this formation, all of which are from the 13th BS. They are approaching landfall, close to their base at 'Kunsan-by-the-Sea' – less romantically referred to as K-8 (Bernard Reck)

MAIN PICTURE *Enlisted type James Lamson works on the top turret guns of an 8th BS B-26. These guns proved to be very effective against anti-aircraft batteries when fired as Invader pulled off the target. Bomber crews found that Chinese gunners would wait until the B-26 had flown over the target before 'opening up'. By training the aircraft's turrets aft, the gunner could pin-point the exact location of the flak battery and zero in on it. The forward-firing guns were controlled by the pilot. Lamson was a talented artist, who painted nose-art on several of the squadron's B-26s (James Lamson)*

INSET *With the war over, the B-26 crews accrued a lot of their flying time on sorties flown between Korea and Japan. This close formation shot of 8th BS Invaders was taken as the bombers flew at extremely low altitude over a small village located near the Japanese base of Yokota (Roy Degan)*

MAIN PICTURE *A lone B-26B taxies out to the main runway after a brief visit to the new 'super base' at Osan-ni (K-55) during the summer of 1953. The aircraft bears the nickname* My Belle *on its nose, but lacks the distinctive fin tip and propeller hub colours associated with either the 3rd or 17th BWs. K-55 boasted just one unit when this photograph was taken – the F-86F-equipped 18th Fighter-Bomber Wing (Kenneth Koon)*

INSET LEFT *Eighth Army commander Lt-Gen James Van Fleet and Ambassador Briggs visit Pusan East in February 1953. This was the home base of the 17th BW, which had just completed a record period of truck destruction. With the Chinese realising that the war was coming to an end, they had tried to gather enough supplies to support an offensive aimed at gaining further ground. However, the B-26 wings had effectively stymied their efforts. Lt-Gen Van Fleet was a firm believer in personally congratulating his forces when they had successfully completed an important task – hence his visit (Bob Tiel)*

INSET RIGHT *A formation of B-26s from the 13th BS head out over North Korea on a SHORAN mission. Note the 'wheel' painted on the vertical stabiliser of the closest Invader. This was the marking worn exclusively by the squadron commander's* CHADWICK *aircraft, although it is unclear whether this is the sixth or seventh example! (Kenneth High)*

CHAPTER FOUR

NOSE ART

RIGHT *Maintenance crews swarm over* Rice Paddy Wagon *at K-8 following the completion of a night sortie in 1952. This was a 17th BW aircraft, and as with a number of other Invaders flown by the wing, it had excellent nose-art (James Wilcox)*

LEFT TORCHY *was a hard-nose B-26B assigned to the 8th BS at Kunsan. These gunships boasted as many as 14 forward-firing machine guns, which made them a most effective weapon against truck convoys and gun emplacements. Most pilots that flew interdiction missions preferred the hard-nose model due to its armament (Robert Fortney)*

BELOW *One of the most realistic paintings to appear on any aircraft during the Korean War was* TOC-SAN, *proudly worn by a B-26C of the 8th BS. Glass-nosed bombers such as this one afforded the bombardier/navigator with the most dangerous, and breathtaking, view of any aircraft type in-theatre. One can only imagine what it must have been like to be sat behind the nose glazing as the Invader barrelled down a deep valley over the tree tops at night, with the only light coming from the moon — or flak! (Robert Fortney)*

INSET *Although the maintenance troops had to work out in the open in some pretty harsh conditions, they had plenty of equipment that gave them easy access to the engines. Indeed, rapid powerplant changes became commonplace at both Pusan East and Kunsan. Little Sheba was yet another example of the great nose-art that proliferated within the 3rd BW. The wing operated almost exclusively from two major bases during the Korean War – Iwakuni and Kunsan. It was also flew from out of Taegu in the early weeks of the conflict (Corky Sumner)*

MAIN PICTURE *AHAULIN was one of the most photographed of all 34th BS B-26s, the squadron having assumed control of the aircraft following its relief of the 728th BS. When the latter unit was ordered back to the USA, it left all of its aircraft behind. The 17th BW finished the war as the sister outfit of the 3rd BW (Will Plentl)*

RIGHT *An 8th BS aircraft was always easy to identify because of its yellow-trimmed vertical stabiliser. It was one of the few UN squadrons to have seen action from the first days of the Korean War to the last. In fact, the last official bombing sortie north of the frontline (on 27 July 1953) was performed by an 8th BS machine. The unit did all of this while flying the same aircraft type that it had first seen action with back in late June 1950. This hard-nose gunship was photographed at Kunsan during the late spring of 1953 (James Council)*

BELOW RIGHT
DEBORAH'S DAD *was also assigned to the 8th BS, which has a lineage that goes all the way back to World War 1. The unit was originally organised at Kelly Field, in Texas, on 31 May 1917, and the Korean War was its third major conflict. Its parent wing (the 3rd BW) was based at Clark AB, in the Philippines, when the call to arms was given in June 1950 (Hans Petermann)*

OPPOSITE *There were a few B-26Bs painted with shark's teeth on the nose, this example hailing from the 13th BS. The full, terrifying, effect of this aircraft at low-level was never fully realised by the North Korean and Chinese troops, for the bulk of the missions flown by the B-26 in-theatre took place at night (Jake Clements)*

Proud crew chief Airman 1st Class Joseph Lobosco poses by his *Bostonians Express* at Kunsan AB. The pilot and navigator are already aboard the aircraft, for they will fly the first night mission as soon as the sun has set. The Invader wings had to have at least one aircraft in each sector at all times so as to combat the movement of enemy convoys southward (Joe Lobosco)

MIDNIGHT RENDEZVOUS *was an unpainted, glass-nose, B-26C. Numerous Invaders within both the 3rd and 17th BW failed to receive the nocturnal all-black paint scheme. The winged eight-ball and yellow trim denote this aircraft's assignment to the 8th BS. When a pilot was struggling with the perennial problem of depth perception on those dark nights over North Korea, it didn't make a whole lot of difference whether he was flying an all-black hard-nose B-26B or a natural metal glass-nose B-26C. Mountains would simply crop up out of nowhere as the crews followed the course of the myriad roads that proliferated 'up north' (Bernard Waller)*

RIGHT *There is a remarkable story behind the name worn by this 13th BS Invader. Mr George Mardikian, the owner of the famous Omar Khayyam's Bar in San Francisco, adopted the unit during the Korean War. He had special cards printed up for its members to carry, and if they happened to be in San Francisco, all they had to do was show the card and drinks were on the house. As a result of this generosity, the unit named one of its gunships after the proprietor. This 'arrangement' was struck during squadron commander Maj Walter King's time in charge at the 13th. OMAR KHAYYAM'S was photographed at Iwakuni AB in the spring of 1951 (Harry Galpin)*

BELOW RIGHT SCOTCH & SODA II *was as much a part of 729th BS folklore as any of its pilots. It was a 'high timer' that flew some of the toughest missions of the war. On one such sortie, pilot Lt Harry Hedlund had his hydraulic lines shot out. Upon landing at Miho with one engine feathered, he then lost his brakes and the gear folded back up. Skidding out of control, Hedlund shot across some railroad tracks and the aircraft suffered severe damage. However, thanks to the efforts of the squadron's maintenance people, it was repaired and went on to fly the 10,000th sortie for the 452nd BW. Here, Lt Guy Brown poses in its cockpit at Miho. Note the low number of mission symbols, which indicates this this photograph was taken during the wing's early days in combat, and long before its major accident (Robert Hansen)*

LEFT Versatile Lady *was undoubtedly the most vividly painted B-26 in the Far East. She was widely photographed, and was involved in several static displays that were arranged for dignitaries visiting the 13th BS at Iwakuni AB. Her assigned pilot was well-known flight leader Capt Tony Curto (Harry Galpin)*

A picture is worth a thousand words! The most prolific artist at K-9 had a unique style that is still easy to spot half a century latter. He also seemed to get better each time he turned out a new masterpiece. Unfortunately, there is no overall view of this aircraft (photographed at Pusan East in early 1953) available to allow its squadron assignment to be ascertained (Will Plentl)

OPPOSITE *Pilot Lt Ray Marzullo poses in front of a 729th BS aircraft at K-9. One of the busiest roads in North Korea was the supply route between Yangdok and Wonsan. During a one-week period in February 1952, 3428 vehicles were sighted on this road. At the other end of the spectrum, the route between Tongchon and Kumhwa witnessed just 200 truck movements over the same period. Both of these routes were regularly patrolled by the 729th BS (Ray Marzullo)*

RIGHT *James Lamson was one of the more talented artists within the 3rd BW, his work gracing the noses of several of the B-26s that flew with the 8th BS. This photograph shows him posing in front of his latest creation, BOOPSIE (James Lamson)*

BELOW RIGHT *Flightcrew from the 8th BS stand by their B-26 prior to climbing aboard. Photographed in the late spring of 1953 at Kunsan, these men are wearing lightweight flying gear. When the weather turned bitterly cold in December/January, insulated flying suits became the order of the day. And even in the warm summer months, the temperatures that crews experienced when flying at 3000 ft over mountains at night often forced them to don extra layers of clothing. Three of the four men in this shot have been identified – gunner Perry Sharp (left), navigator Lt John Sidirourgos (second from left) and pilot Lt Ed Fay (far right) (John Sidirourgos)*

MAIN PICTURE *To the average American, LSMFT stood for 'Lucky Strike Mighty Fine Tobacco'. But the artwork on this B-26 stood for something completely different – 'Loaded Spare Might Fly Tonight'. The 55-gallon drums and pierced-steel planking indicate that this B-26 was parked on an older section of Pusan East air base. Photographed in the spring of 1953, the aircraft features the red trim of the 37th BS (Dexter Martin)*

INSET *The white-trimmed B-26s of the 730th BS flew an unusually high number of daylight bombing missions during its time in Korea. By the late summer of 1951, these missions began to taper off due to a lack of good targets. The B-29s had by then levelled all of the strategic targets in North Korea, so the B-26s were used instead to break up Chinese troop concentrations. The latter mission effectively prevented the enemy from launching a new ground offensive. B-26C* MAXIMUM EFFORT *flew its fair share of these missions with the 730th BS (Robert Stoner)*

THE OSAKA STAGE *was Capt Del Gosser's regular aircraft, its nose-art depicting four crewmen flying in a most precarious manner. The aircraft was assigned to the 90th BS, which was the 3rd BW's third squadron. It took over the 731st BS's aircraft at Kunsan in July 1951 after the latter unit had fulfilled its reserve commitment of one year. The 90th's lineage dated all the way back to 20 August 1917, when it was formed as the 90th Aero Squadron. This photograph was taken in late 1952 at Kunsan AB (Clarence Klenk)*

OPPOSITE *The 13th BS possessed a large number of hard-nose B-26Bs, with BROWN NOSE being one of the more famous. A well known fixture at Kunsan, it survived many combat missions. Fitted with 14 forward-firing guns, the hard-nose B-26 was the perfect weapon for destroying truck convoys. The 13th was well versed in working under the flares dropped by the C-47 'Fireflies' along the many roads that criss-crossed North Korea (Leroy Bain)*

LEFT *Little Debbie was also the work of artist Jim Lamson, this aircraft being assigned to the 13th BS late on in the war. During this period, the 3rd BW passed the 25,000th sortie mark, and it was well on its way to attaining its final tally of 31,000 when this photograph was taken. The 3rd had flown its first 10,000 sorties by 18 June 1951, and during this time it had dropped over 13,000 tons of explosives (Joe Lobosco)*

BELOW LEFT *A pilot and crew chief from the 17th BW pose in front of the wing commander's personal Invader* THIS IS IT *– note the 17th's emblem painted beside the name. Col Gordon Timmons was the wing CO at the time. Whenever Chinese logistics personnel increased their efforts to re-supply the frontline force, the 17th matched it. For example, during a two-week period ending 22 February 1953, the wing accounted for 822 vehicles destroyed (Dexter Martin)*

B-26B My Mary Lou *was photographed at Pusan East in May 1953. It survived the war in fine shape, and was eventually bought and restored in the 1990s by warbird enthusiasts in Texas. The Invader was assigned to the 95th BS whilst performing the night interdiction mission in Korea. The artist did an outstanding job when applying this masterpiece (Bob Tiel)*

MAIN PICTURE *Lt Robert Tiel poses in front of his B-26C at Pusan East in February 1953. When the 452nd BW finished its tour in Korea, the wing was replaced by the 17th BW. The former's 730th BS became the 95th BS accordingly, and this photograph shows the squadron's 'kicking mule' emblem to good effect. The 730th's colour was blue, as shown on Tiel's scarf (Robert Tiel)*

INSET *A second* My Mary Lou *also flew with the 13th BS. Its navigator, 2Lt Bernard Reck, later flew F-105 Thunderchiefs in Vietnam (Bernard Reck)*

INSET *This B-26C saw much action during a lengthy frontline tour. It had originally arrived in-theatre with the 728th BS/452nd BW in October of 1950, and carried the name* The Golden Bear *as a reflection of its West Coast roots. By the time this photograph was taken the aircraft had been passed on the 34th BS at Pusan East. The latter unit had received all of the 728th's aircraft when the reserve's completed their tour (James Wilcox)*

MAIN PICTURE *Lt Col Robert Fortney's* THE SIXTH CHADWICK *sits on the Kunsan ramp between sorties in mid-1952. This aircraft was sent to the boneyard after a young pilot within the 13th BS carried out two barrel rolls in it. The wings were so badly stressed during the impromptu aerobatics session that the aircraft was subsequently declared a write-off (Leroy Bain)*

Appendices

INVADER STATISTICS

452nd Bomb Wing
(AF Reserve Unit from Long Beach, California*)

sorties flown – 14,000
bomb tonnage – 22,300
0.5-in rounds fired – 7,000,000
napalm bombs dropped – 50,000

* these figures are incomplete and do not show all the totals for a wide variety of ordnance delivered.

The 452nd was involved in combat for only 18 of the 37 months that the war lasted. The wing officially flew its first combat mission over North Korea on 27 October 1950. and was officially relieved from combat on 10 May 1952

3rd Bomb Wing
(25 June 1950 to 27 July 1953*)

vehicles destroyed – 31,000
artillery pieces destroyed – 208
locomotives destroyed – 332
enemy aircraft destroyed – 4
railcars destroyed – 2920
rail cuts – 845
tanks knocked out – 24
road cuts – 816
bridges knocked out – 114
buildings destroyed – 531

1126 Days of Combat, during which 33,220 daylight and night sorties were flown

* these figures originated with the 3rd Bomb Group's Intelligence Officer (31 July 1953), and include the 8th, 13th, 90th and 731st Bomb Squadrons' records

DOUGLAS B-26B INVADER

Powerplant
two Pratt & Whitney R-2800-79 Double Wasp engines, rated at 2000 hp (1491 kW) each

Performance
maximum speed, 355 mph (571 km/h)
initial climb 2000 ft (610 m) per minute
service ceiling 22,100 ft (6736 m)
range with maximum bombload 1400 miles (2253 km)

Weights
empty, typically 22,362 lb (10,143 kg)
normal loaded 35,000 lb (15,876 kg)
maximum overload 41,800 lb (18,960 kg)

Dimensions
Span: 70 ft 0 in (21.34 m)
Length: 50 ft 8 in (15.44 m)
Height: 18 ft 6 in (5.64 m)

Armament
ten 0.5-in (12.7 mm) Colt-Browning M-3 machine guns, six fixed in nose and two each in dorsal and ventral turrets; internal bombload of 4000 lbs (1814kg), supplemented by load of up to 2000 lbs (907 kg)

UNIT CITATION

The following Distinguished Unit Citation was awarded to the 3rd Bomb Wing on 23 February 1951 for its heroic efforts during the early days of the war when it was the only B-26 outfit in theatre, and operating with only two squadrons. It is quoted verbatim:

Headquarters
Far East Air Forces
APO 925

23 February 1951

CITATION

The 3rd Bombardment Group(L) is cited for extraordinary heroism and distinguished service in action against an enemy of the United States during the period 27 June 1950 to 31 July 1950. Showing a high state of training and combat readiness, the 3rd Bomb Group, after the communist attack on South Korea, made immediate and effective transition from training to combat status, and, between 27 June 1950 and 31 July 1950, with limited facilities, accumulated a total of 672 effective day and night combat sorties.

Utilising B-26 attack bombers which were developed during World War 2, the 3rd Bomb Group launched its initial attack against the enemies of the United Nations on 27 June 1950, only two days after the beginning of active resistance against the communist aggressors in Korea. Two days later, on 29 June 1950, it attacked the North Korean Airfield at Pyongyang with excellent results, thus making the first United Nations strike at the communist forces above the 38th Parallel.

The inherent versatility of the B-26 aircraft was fully exploited by the able and intrepid airmen of this organisation, the type of missions flown having included interdiction, armed reconnaissance, escort, night intruder, night attack, close support and submarine patrol. All of these missions were subject to enemy air and ground attack, and many of the aircraft from the 3rd Bomb Group were shot down. The tactics which were used included medium altitude precision bombing, glide bombing and low level attack as was most appropriate; however, tactics were often dictated by severe weather conditions with which the 3rd effectively contended.

As a result of the co-ordinated and sustained attacks by the 3rd Bomb Group, the enemy lost 42 tanks, 163 vehicles, 65 bridges, 12 marshalling yards, 14 supply dumps, 39 locomotives and numerous items of rolling stock. An estimated 5225 personnel casualties were also inflicted upon the enemy.

Repeated acts of valour and gallantry have marked the aerial accomplishments of the 3rd Bomb Group, yet only through the extended and continuous efforts of each individual officer and airman was it possible to achieve its high degree of effectiveness. Although they suffered severe losses of personnel and equipment during those early days of combat operations, the morale and effectiveness of the Group was sustained at a high level. The enviable combat record compiled by the 3rd Bomb Group reflects great credit upon its individual members, the Far East Air Forces, and the United States Air Force.

Douglas A-26B Invader

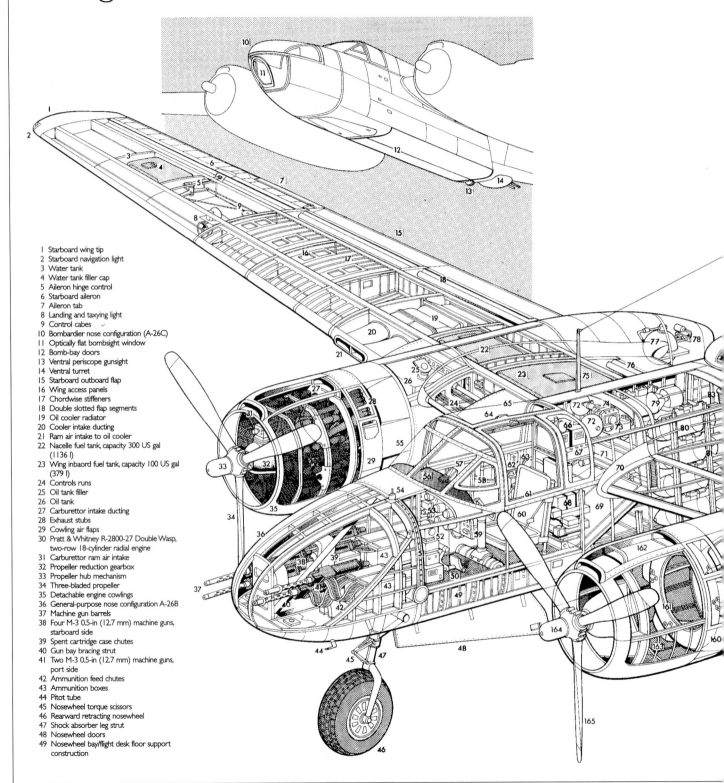

1   Starboard wing tip
2   Starboard navigation light
3   Water tank
4   Water tank filler cap
5   Aileron hinge control
6   Starboard aileron
7   Aileron tab
8   Landing and taxying light
9   Control cabes
10 Bombardier nose configuration (A-26C)
11 Optically flat bombsight window
12 Bomb-bay doors
13 Ventral periscope gunsight
14 Ventral turret
15 Starboard outboard flap
16 Wing access panels
17 Chordwise stiffeners
18 Double slotted flap segments
19 Oil cooler radiator
20 Cooler intake ducting
21 Ram air intake to oil cooler
22 Nacelle fuel tank, capacity 300 US gal
    (1136 l)
23 Wing inbaord fuel tank, capacity 100 US gal
    (379 l)
24 Controls runs
25 Oil tank filler
26 Oil tank
27 Carburettor intake ducting
28 Exhaust stubs
29 Cowling air flaps
30 Pratt & Whitney R-2800-27 Double Wasp,
    two-row 18-cylinder radial engine
31 Carburettor ram air intake
32 Propeller reduction gearbox
33 Propeller hub mechanism
34 Three-bladed propeller
35 Detachable engine cowlings
36 General-purpose nose configuration A-26B
37 Machine gun barrels
38 Four M-3 0.5-in (12.7 mm) machine guns,
    starboard side
39 Spent cartridge case chutes
40 Gun bay bracing strut
41 Two M-3 0.5-in (12.7 mm) machine guns,
    port side
42 Ammunition feed chutes
43 Ammunition boxes
44 Pitot tube
45 Nosewheel torque scissors
46 Rearward retracting nosewheel
47 Shock absorber leg strut
48 Nosewheel doors
49 Nosewheel bay/flight desk floor support
    construction

50 Rudder pedals
51 Interchangeable nose joint bulkhead
52 Autopilot controls
53 Back of instrument panel
54 Fixed foresight
55 Windscreen panels
56 Instrument panel shroud
57 Reflector sight
58 Clear vision panel
59 Control column
60 Pilot's seat
61 Pilot's side window panel/entry hatch
62 Bomb release controls
63 Bombardier/navigator's seat
64 Canopy hatch handles
65 Bombardier/navigator's side canopy/entry
   hatch
66 Oxygen regulator
67 Radio racks
68 Radio receivers and transmitters

69 Bomb-bay armoured roof panel
70 Wing root fillet
71 Armoured wing spar bulkhead
72 Hydraulic accumulators
73 Air filter
74 De-icing valve
75 Aerial mast
76 Double slotted flap inboard section
77 Wing de-icing fluid reservoir
78 De-icing fluid pump

106 Fin rib construction
107 Starboard tailplane
108 Starboard elevator
109 Fin leading edge
110 Aerial cables
111 Fin tip fairing
112 Fabric covered rudder construction
113 Rudder tab
114 Trim tab control
115 Rudder hinge post
116 Tail navigation lights
117 Elevator tab
118 Port elevator
119 Port tailplane construction
120 Elevator control horns
121 Tailplane root fillet
122 Fin/tailplane fixing frame
123 Rear fuselage construction
124 Oxygen bottles
125 Rear fuselage construction joint bulkhead
126 Turret control amplifier
127 Turret covers
128 Ventral turret control mechanism
129 Two 0.5-in (12.7 mm) machine guns
130 Port nacelle tailcone
131 Aft nacelle construction
132 Engine fire extinguishers

Mike Badrocke

86 Turret mechanism
87 Ammunition boxes
88 Port aft bomb rack, three 100-lb (45 kg) HE
   bombs
89 Inboard double-slotted flap
90 Gunner's bomb-bay entry hatch
91 Oxygen cylinders
92 Life raft
93 Gunner's canopy cover
94 Ditching hatch
95 Upper periscope sight
96 Periscope eyepiece
97 Turret controls
98 Oxygen bottles
99 Gunner's armoured bulkhead

133 Main undercarriage wheel well
134 Outboard double slotted flaps
135 Flap hinge links
136 Wing rear spar
137 Aileron tab
138 Port aileron
139 Fabric-covered aileron construction
140 Port wing tip
141 Port navigation light
142 Wing rib construction
143 Leading edge stiffeners
144 Aileron hinge control
145 Landing and taxiing lamp housing
146 Wing front spar
147 Fluid de-iced leading edge
148 Mainwheel doors
149 Main undercarriage door link mechanism
150 Retraction jack
151 Main undercarriage leg
152 Rearward-retracting mainwheel
153 Access panel
154 Nacelle fuel tank, capacity 300 US gal
   (1136 l)
155 Oil cooler ram air intake
156 Oil tank filler cap
157 Engine compartment bulkhead/firewall
158 Engine-mounting struts
159 Exhaust ducts
160 Cowling cooling air flaps

79 Starboard bomb rack, five 100-lb (45 kg) HE
   bombs
80 Port bomb rack, five 100-lb (45 kg) HE
   bombs
81 Bomb launcher rails
82 Rear wing spar bulkhead
83 Turret drive motor
84 Upper remotely-controlled gun turret
85 Two M-3 0.5-in (12.7 mm) machine guns

100 Ventral turret ammunition boxes
101 Cabin heater
102 D/F loop antenna fairing
103 Fin root fillet
104 Tailplane control cables
105 Cable pulleys

161 Engine-mounting bulkhead
162 Carburettor intake ducting
163 Cowling construction
164 Propeller hub mechanism
165 Three-bladed propeller

B-26 Invader Patch Gallery

1

2

3

4

5

6

7

8

9

10

11